PSYCHOLOGY SQUARED

PSYCHOLOGY SQUARE^D

100 CONCEPTS YOU SHOULD KNOW

CHRISTOPHER STERLING
AND DANIEL FRINGS

WITH A CONTRIBUTION BY ELIZABETH J. NEWTON

METRO BOOKS
New York

METRO BOOKS
New York

An Imprint of Sterling Publishing
1166 Avenue of the Americas
New York NY 10036

METRO BOOKS and the distinctive Metro Books logo are trademarks of Sterling Publishing Co., Inc.

This book was designed, conceived, and produced by
Quantum Books Limited
6 Blundell Street
London N7 9BH
United Kingdom

Publisher: Kerry Enzor
Editorial and Design: Pikaia Imaging
Editor: Anna Southgate
Design: Dave Jones
Illustration: Tim Brown and Dave Jones
Production Manager: Zarni Win

ISBN 978-1-4351-6243-3

For information about custom editions, special sales, and premium and corporate purchases,
please contact Sterling Special Sales at 800-805-5489 or specialsales@sterlingpublishing.com.

Printed in China by Toppan Leefung Printing Limited

2 4 6 8 10 9 7 5 3 1

www.sterlingpublishing.com

Cover image courtesy of http://thegraphicsfairy.com

Contents

INTRODUCTION 6

1 PSYCHOLOGY IN CONTEXT 10

2 BIOLOGICAL INFLUENCES 34

3 LIFE-SPAN PSYCHOLOGY 58

4 SOCIAL BEHAVIOR 82

5 COGNITION: OUR WORLD VIEW 106

6 LEARNING & EXPERTISE 130

7 MOTIVATION, STRESS, & EMOTION . . . 154

8 GROUPS & INDIVIDUALS 178

9 MENTAL HEALTH 202

10 APPLICATIONS & GUIDANCE 226

GLOSSARY 250

INDEX 252

Introduction

An interest in the human mind dates back millennia, from the ancients in China, through India and Persia to Egypt and Greece. Driven initially by a need to understand the causes and consequences of abnormal behavior, this interest developed into an identifiable academic discipline in ancient Greece.

Modern-day psychology—with its emphasis on collecting information directly from the participants of a study and subjecting the results to rigorous analysis—dates back to Wilhelm Wundt's Institute for Experimental Psychology in Leipzig in the 1880s. Interest spread rapidly to other parts of Europe and North America through the 20th century.

The purpose of this book is to outline what psychologists now know about people's thoughts and behavior. The material falls quite naturally into ten chapters, starting with a consideration of contextual issues such as the relative effects of nature and nurture and the ethics of psychological investigation, and finishing with ways in which psychology can help people improve their lives. In between, there are key chapters on how we humans develop over the life span, how we make sense of the world through our senses and powers of reasoning, and how we relate to others in socially and emotionally appropriate ways.

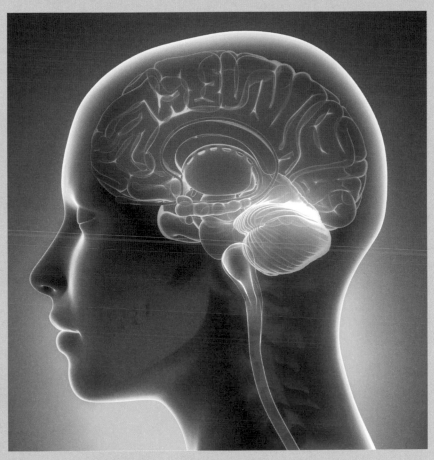

The human brain. The seat of the mind and the most advanced
piece of technology in the known universe.

Each of the ten chapters identifies a further ten key topics. For example, the chapter on social behavior covers attitudes, conformity, and social identity while the chapter on motivation, emotion, and stress identifies the needs that drive us, feelings of anger and love, and how stress affects us. Each topic is introduced and the current state of knowledge summarized using accessible language and an illustration to clarify or extend the information in the text.

We hope that, as you read this book, you become as fascinated by the diversity of content as we are. If you are interested in why people do what they do, there is much to satisfy and arouse your curiosity. If you are intrigued by the relationship between brain and behavior, you will find much to stimulate your interest. And if you wonder about how psychology influences broader issues, look into topics such as intergroup contact and mental health.

The last hundred years have seen an explosion of psychological knowledge, from simple experiments in perception and memory to the use of computer simulations, brain scanning, and sophisticated statistics to try and answer research questions in developmental, social, and cognitive psychology. Nevertheless, there is still some way to go and it increasingly appears that we are only at the stage of knowing what we need to know.

Chris Sterling and Daniel Frings

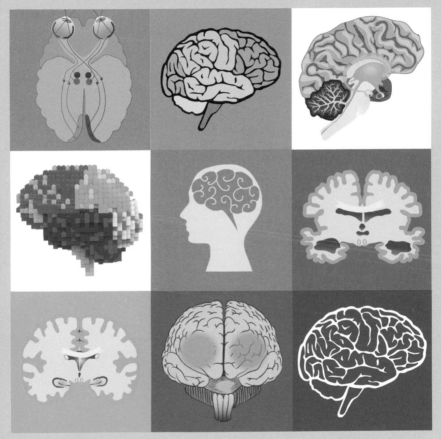

Among the subjects covered in this book are the following (as illustrated from top left to bottom right): modularity of mind; brain anatomy; autism; structure of the mind; scientific method; Alzheimer's disease; the healthy brain; brain plasticity; biological influences.

PSYCHOLOGY IN CONTEXT

1

Many of us imagine a typical shrink when we hear the word "psychology." We picture a therapy room, a couch, books, and charts. Of course, therapy has a role to play, as we'll discuss later, but the discipline is more complex than that, and includes a great deal of theoretical development as well as practical application.

Scholars have been studying how and why we think and behave the way we do for many hundreds of years, in places as far and wide as ancient Egypt, Persia, Greece, China, and India. However, psychology as a science is a relatively recent development.

Psychology draws on a wealth of other disciplines, embracing ideas for biology, computer sciences, linguistics, and philosophy, to name but a few. The benefits and tensions of such a wide scope can be found throughout this book, but are highlighted particularly in

Continues overleaf

the discussions on scientific method and combined disciplines that follow.

It is important to note that psychology does not exist in a vacuum: Historical events also have a role to play. The influence of World War II and other large-scale events, for example, cannot be underestimated. In particular, we discuss what constitutes "ethical" and "unethical" research. We also consider the most appropriate ways to understand and study psychology. Is an experiment-based quantitative approach best? Or does a more, discussion-based qualitative approach yield better results?

Perhaps the most fundamental issues discussed here are about free will and consciousness. Just how much of our behavior is automatic? To what degree are we influenced by our genetic makeup?

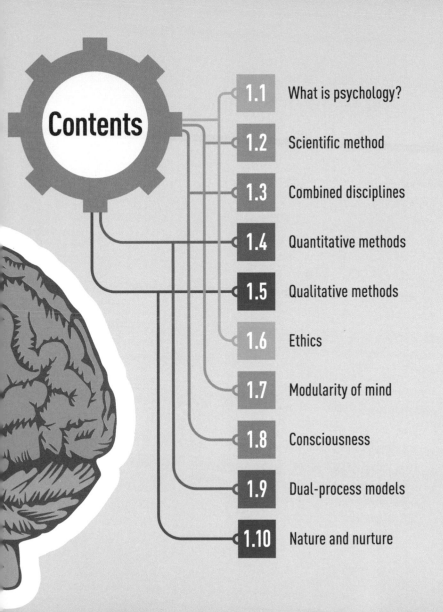

Contents

1.1 What is psychology?

1.2 Scientific method

1.3 Combined disciplines

1.4 Quantitative methods

1.5 Qualitative methods

1.6 Ethics

1.7 Modularity of mind

1.8 Consciousness

1.9 Dual-process models

1.10 Nature and nurture

1.1 What is psychology?

Psychology is the study of human behavior. Its aim is to find out what makes us tick. But why should anyone bother?

By studying our behavior—how we respond to different situations and in different conditions—psychologists want to learn more about the mental processes that influence our actions. Essentially, they want to know what we are thinking.

Many approaches to psychology exist. For some time, the dominant approach was **behaviorism**. This focused on the idea that behavior is learnt through pairing a stimulus (a given event) with a response (the outcome of that event), be it reward or punishment. Today, approaches are primarily **cognitive**. Psychologists argue that it is the processing of information in this stimulus-response relationship that is of interest. How do our thoughts lead to the automatic responses we make, and what role does memory play in forming those thoughts?

Understanding these processes allows psychologists to help people understand and improve their own psychological lives. To this end, psychologists work directly with people in areas as diverse as personnel selection, the treatment of mental illness, and child development.

Through this easy-to-read guide you will discover 100 key concepts in the field of psychology. Together they present an insight into the discipline, showing not only how, but why the study of human behavior is fundamental to all aspects of our daily lives.

There are more than 100,000 licensed psychologists in the United States.

What do you see?

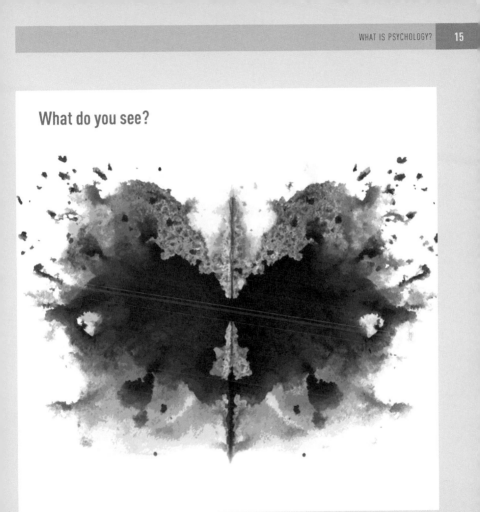

Devised in the 1920s, the Rorschach inkblot test involves an individual interpreting a range of near symmetrical abstract images. Psychologists use the results to assess personality.

1.2 Scientific method

Psychology has close relationships with other sciences and draws heavily on scientific method to advance knowledge.

Many academic disciplines concern themselves with human behavior. Literary analysis provides fascinating and profound insights into the human condition. Sociology and human geography tell us how societies form, interact, and adapt to the environment in which they live. History tracks this development over millennia.

Psychology differs significantly from these disciplines in the following ways. Primarily, it deals with people first hand on a day-to-day basis. Information about what those people do is collected directly and methodically. Objectivity and verification are paramount. There is no room for a psychologist's own opinions and theories when collecting, analyzing, and interpreting data. For an investigation to have credibility, exactly the same results must emerge if the method is replicated by an independent researcher. Finally, the validity of the study—its methods, rationale, and interpretation—must be open to scrutiny. All of this proves that psychology draws heavily on the **scientific method** to advance knowledge.

Psychology's scientific roots are undeniable. The discipline is anchored in the biological sciences and has close links to medical and social sciences, too (see opposite). The beauty of these relationships is that they are two-way. Many aspects of psychology are informed by other sciences, and yet it informs them in return.

A placebo is a false treatment that may have the same effect as the real treatment, simply because of a patient's expectations.

Psychology and the sciences

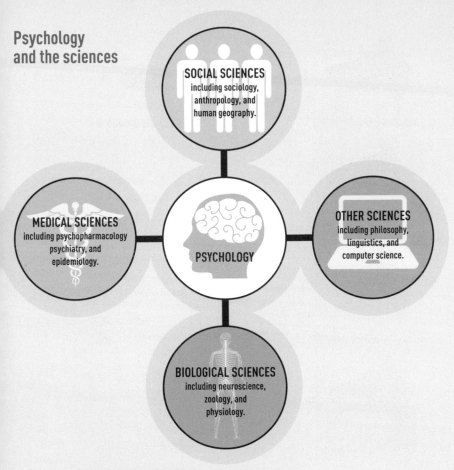

Psychology and its relationship with other disciplines. Ties with the social sciences contribute to our understanding of how people relate to each other and society as a whole.

1.3 Combined disciplines

What we learn from psychology is of little use in isolation. For the bigger picture, we must combine it with evidence from other disciplines.

Psychology is informed by related work in other disciplines. These often ask the same questions using different methods and different assumptions.

Consider object recognition, as demonstrated by a simulation model by the computer scientist, David Marr (see Topic 5.2). The model was based on physiological evidence collected by David Hubel and Torsten Wiesel and the experimental psychology of the Gestalt school. Further work in experimental psychology and neuropsychology showed that there is a distinction between the processing of objects and that of faces. Evidence from brain scanning is helping to clarify this hypothesized distinction.

Another example relates to language. Linguists and philosophers explore the structure of language and how it conveys meaning. Psychologists, however, use behavioral experiments to tell us how we learn and use language, supported by evidence from electrical activity in the brain. Combined with research by zoologists, psycholinguists, and animal behaviorists, we are able to build a more complete understanding of human language and how it relates to the communication systems of other animals.

Brain scanning using magnetic resonance imaging (MRI) provides a picture of structural damage and brain activity in real time.

In using evidence from diverse sources, we can be more confident that our understanding is secure. This combining of disciplines is known as **disciplinary convergence**.

A multidisciplinary approach

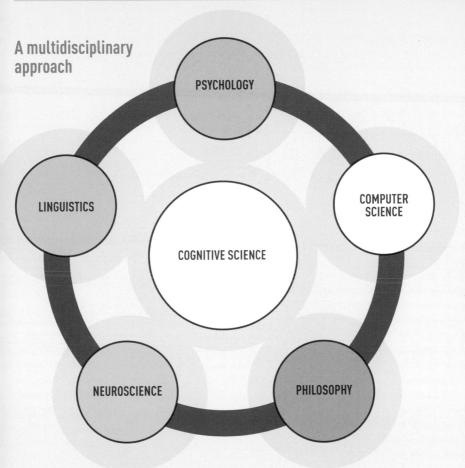

The subdiscipline of cognitive science exemplifies this combining of disciplines. It is a collaboration of psychologists, neuroscientists, philosophers, linguists, and computer scientists.

1.4 Quantitative methods

Sometimes the triggers for our behavior are revealed through the rigorous analysis of results from surveys and experiments.

Quantitative methods ask: "What are the factors that cause or predict behavior?" We can apply this question to anything from driving performance to language development. The defining feature of this approach is that observations made must be **quantifiable**—the number of errors made when driving or the number of words in a child's vocabulary.

Experiments can help to answer the question, particularly when one or more factors are manipulated. For example, we might give different groups of people different volumes of alcohol and compare the number of errors they make in a driving simulator. This experimental method has the major advantage of establishing a cause: If errors increase with the amount of alcohol, we can conclude that alcohol causes a deterioration in performance.

For practical or ethical reasons, the experimental method is not always used. In such cases, a correlational study may be more appropriate. Say we want to identify lifetime factors that predict alcohol abuse. We might survey people's alcohol consumption, but also consider stress, weekly income, relations with a drink problem, and so on. We can use statistics to identify which factors are the best predictors.

The Mogul Emperor Akbar (1542–1605) ordered an experiment that deprived children of spoken language. They emerged using signs but not language.

Unlike quantitative methods, correlational methods do not establish cause, only likelihood. Nevertheless both are invaluable tools in the psychologist's kit bag.

Quantitative results

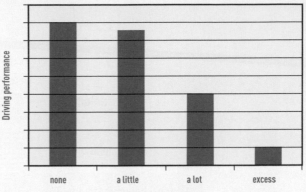

This analysis compares results of different treatments, in this case, the effect of different amounts of alcohol on driving performance.

This analysis looks at the association between degree of life stress and weekly alcohol consumption.

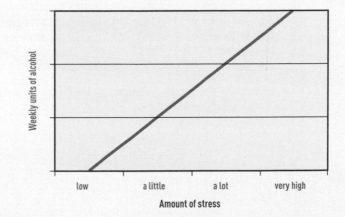

These graphs illustrate two types of quantitative result. The results need to meet a statistical criterion of at least 95% reliability. Any result not meeting this criterion is rejected.

1.5 Qualitative methods

According to qualitative psychologists, it's not just what you say, but how you say it that matters when analyzing behavior.

Grounded theory considers recurring themes and how these might provide insight into existing theories about behavior.

Although much psychology relies on quantitative methods (see Topic 1.4), this is not the only approach. Qualitative methods focus on rich data sources such as interviews, and attempt to understand the individual experience in the context of the here and now.

Qualitative psychologists approach the study of psychology from a different perspective. They reject notions of **positivism**—the view that reality can be known and scientifically observed. Instead, they adopt postmodern perspectives to understanding. They see all data, and particularly language, as a reflection of reality, but not reality itself. Qualitative researchers therefore recognize that any data or idea is subject to multiple interpretations.

The argument is that all knowledge is the result of social interaction, is historically bound, and influenced by the language used to describe it. One approach, discourse analysis, focuses on what people say, and how they say it. By analyzing cultural references and archetypes used, the deeper meanings behind seemingly simple phrases and gestures, links are made with broader social themes.

With its focus on language and interviews, qualitative psychology may seem to conflict with quantitative methods. However, many researchers use both, applying the appropriate tool to the appropriate level of problem.

Focus groups

Early methods of qualitative psychology, such as grounded theory, gained traction in the 1960s. These methods used data sources such as one-on-one interviews or focus groups, and continue to do so today.

1.6 Ethics

Psychologists are bound by a strict code of conduct—both beside the couch and in the lab.

Psychologists are provided with guidance on ethics. In the United States, this is established by the American Psychological Associate; in Britain, by the British Psychological Society.

Although codes of conduct vary from country to country, in general they are based on principles such as:

- Respect: Appreciating the dignity and worth of all
- Competence: Working to one's competences only, and valuing the maintenance and development of these
- Responsibility: To clients, the public, the profession, and science
- Integrity: Being honest, accurate, and fair with others.

For research, the key principles are as follows:
- Respect for autonomy, privacy and dignity
- Scientific integrity
- Social responsibility
- A duty to maximize benefit and minimize harm.

Research guidelines draw, in part, on worldwide research standards such as the Declaration of Helsinki (1964).

Typically, research conducted on both human and animal participants are reviewed by an ethics committee (in the United States known as an Institutional Review Board, IRB). Their involvement ensures that these principles are met before any research is undertaken.

Developed for the medical profession, the Declaration of Helsinki sets out principles of ethics for human research. The concept emerged, in part, as a result of the highly unethical research on humans uncovered during the Nuremberg trials (1945–46).

1.7 Modularity of mind

Think of your brain as a collection of separate systems that constantly interact with one another.

Even at a superficial level we think of processes like memory, language, and perception as being relatively distinct from one another. Modularity of mind is the idea that these processes are, in fact, independent modules. The key feature is that, although they interact with each other, each has its own set of processes (see also, Topic 2.1).

There is evidence to support this. For example, case studies of people with brain damage show that an individual can be densely amnesic, yet retain all perceptual abilities and an undamaged language ability. In contrast there are cases where the language function is impaired, but perception and memory are unaffected.

Memory can be divided into different subsystems, each of which is a module in its own right (see Topic 5.3). Similarly, we can distinguish between language comprehension and language production modules. Perception divides naturally into visual and auditory modules.

Some kinds of brain damage lead to a loss of knowledge about living things, but not about nonliving things, and vice-versa. This suggests modular organization.

In order for us to function fully other, non-modular, processes operate across these modules. Focused attention, for example, is required for both language comprehension and memory. The same applies to executive function, responsible for planning, switching between tasks and monitoring performance (see Topic 5.5).

The visual projection pathway

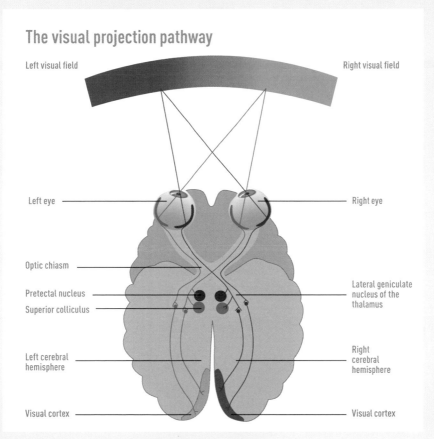

Left visual field

Right visual field

Left eye

Right eye

Optic chiasm

Lateral geniculate
nucleus of the
thalamus

Pretectal nucleus

Superior colliculus

Left cerebral
hemisphere

Right
cerebral
hemisphere

Visual cortex

Visual cortex

The modularized visual system has elements distributed throughout
the brain. Visual information enters through the eyes and travels via
the lateral geniculate to the visual cortex in both hemispheres.

1.8 Consciousness

Delving into the conscious mind reveals the likely existence of different kinds of consciousness.

The behaviorists of the 20th century dismissed consciousness as a distraction from the real problems of understanding behavior. Nevertheless, observations in neuropsychology have shed some light on the subject. Examining people with brain damage, it would seem that different kinds of consciousness exist.

Reports of people with dense amnesia, such as the celebrated amnesic H.M. (1926–2008), suggest that they are aware of the world around them and able to comment on it. They are able to hold conversations and are, in all obvious ways, fully conscious. This kind of consciousness is called **phenomenological consciousness**. However, amnesics like H.M. lack the ability actively to search their memories. Similarly, people with frontal lobe damage seem unable actively to set goals, plan a course of action to achieve those goals, and monitor progress. These types of deficit suggest a different, more active kind of consciousness.

The amnesic C.W. lived in a constant state of immediacy, convinced throughout the day that he had only just woken up.

Phenomenological awareness does not seem necessary for carrying out tasks that are highly overlearned and automatized. Thus we are perfectly able to find our way to work in the morning without planning and often arrive unaware of what happened on the way there. On the other hand, if there is a traffic incident, we need to call on the more active kind of consciousness to plan a new route.

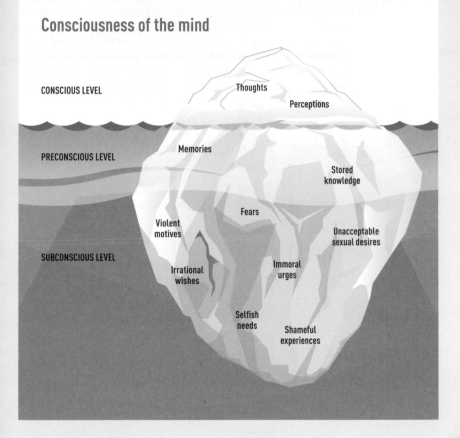

Consciousness of the mind

CONSCIOUS LEVEL

Thoughts

Perceptions

PRECONSCIOUS LEVEL

Memories

Stored knowledge

Fears

Violent motives

Unacceptable sexual desires

SUBCONSCIOUS LEVEL

Irrational wishes

Immoral urges

Selfish needs

Shameful experiences

Freud's model of the mind in terms of the conscious, the preconscious, and the subconscious. Each type of consciousness refers to a level of awareness, influence on behavior, and accessibility.

1.9 Dual-process models

Do we make all of our decisions consciously, or are we just coasting along in automatic mode?

Dual-process models show that processes can take place via different routes or methods. In psychology, this usually demonstrates our behavior as being influenced via a reflective route and/or an automatic route.

A reflective route is characterized by conscious thought and is relatively slow. An automatic route is subconscious and relatively fast. It is often referred to as **implicit processing**. For example, attitudes about people from different ethnic backgrounds can be held explicitly: We verbalize them internally and express them publically. They can also be held implicitly as associations of value concepts such as good and bad and category labels such as black and white.

Automatic processes can be subject to biases: Research by scientists such as John Bargh has shown that priming concepts in one domain can affect unrelated domains. For example, holding a hot coffee may lead a person to rate an individual as warm; a person identifying words associated with being elderly may walk more slowly.

Dual-process models have been applied to numerous areas of cognitive and social psychology. Examples of a dual-process approach in this book include a person's susceptibility to persuasion (see Topic 4.4), forming stereotypes (see Topic 4.3), and forming attitudes (see Topic 4.1).

Dual-process approaches suggest we behave "consciously" only a small proportion of the time.

Doughnut deliberations

The same stimulus or situation can elicit different responses, depending on whether we act in automatic or reflective mode. In this case, the decision is whether or not to eat a doughnut.

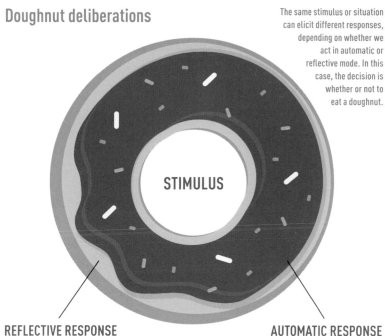

STIMULUS

REFLECTIVE RESPONSE

If I reflect on it, I consider the number of calories, that I am not really hungry, and decline it.

AUTOMATIC RESPONSE

If I behave automatically, I just go ahead and eat it without thinking.

Dual-process accounts argue that sometimes we process using a fast, often unconscious, automatic mode and sometimes using a slower, more reasoned and reflective mode.

1.10 Nature and nurture

Is everything we do determined by the genes in our bodies? Or are we driven by our experience of the world around us?

A long-running debate in psychology is the extent to which our thoughts and behaviors are influenced by nature and nurture. Nature involves our genetic makeup, or innate traits and tendencies. Nurture is the influence of the physical and social environment, and of experience.

Behaviorists favor the concept of the *tabula rasa* (a blank slate). They argue that an individual can be shaped to behave in any way given the correct schedule of punishment and reinforcement. Concepts such as evolutionary psychology promote biological determinism, where behavior is dictated by genetic factors following years of evolution.

Evidence suggests a mixture of the two is most likely. In studies of separated twins similarities are seen in areas such as likelihood of depression, personality, political orientation, and music taste. High levels of genetic similarity can be linked to such traits and behavior. However, in such cases there is still a large amount of variance unaccounted for, which could indicate the role played by environment. The situation is complicated further, since environmental factors have been shown to affect the way genes express themselves and, consequently, influence us.

Given the evidence, perhaps we should be asking a different question. Instead of considering nature vs. nurture, we should be looking at the ways in which the two interact.

We each have around 24,000 genes. We are also affected by our environment 24 hours a day.

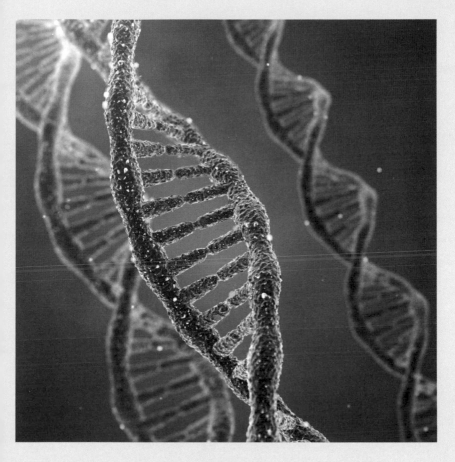

Are we held captive by our genes? The study of the way nature and nurture interact begins to inform us of the extent to which our genes dictate our behavior, inform debates about culpability for one's actions, and explores what exactly we mean by free will.

BIOLOGICAL INFLUENCES

2

Psychology is all about our behavior and its relationship with the workings of the brain. As such, the discipline is firmly anchored in the biological sciences. Although human psychology is the primary concern, investigations of animal brains and behavior are also essential.

This chapter begins with the idea that our behavior stems from a number of distinct systems or modules in the brain—language, memory, and perception, for example. Each of these is controlled by one or more anatomical structures. To examine this more closely we look at the anatomy of the brain and outline its primary structures and their major functions. What exactly do they do?

Continues overleaf

Progressing to the nervous system, we find out how these modules are controlled. This complex network of neurons connects the brain to the rest of the body, transmitting messages from one neuron to the next. It is amazing to think that, essentially, much of our behavior starts at this tiny, cellular level. Certain shifts in behavior relate directly to changes in the strength of the connections between these neurons.

A broader view of the relationship between the brain and behavior follows. What roles do hormones, genes, and the environment play in our behavior? Finally, we look at human behavior in the context of evolution, and the degree to which our understanding of human behavior is informed by that of other animals.

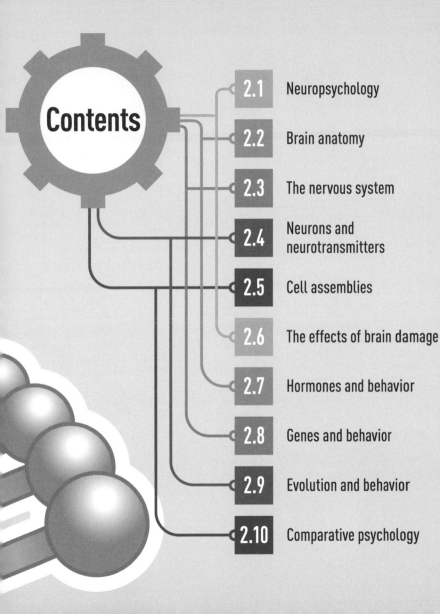

Contents

2.1 Neuropsychology

2.2 Brain anatomy

2.3 The nervous system

2.4 Neurons and neurotransmitters

2.5 Cell assemblies

2.6 The effects of brain damage

2.7 Hormones and behavior

2.8 Genes and behavior

2.9 Evolution and behavior

2.10 Comparative psychology

2.1 Neuropsychology

What exactly is the link between our brain, its various functions, and our behavior?

During the 19th century scientists known as phrenologists, argued that certain human traits, such as ambition and cunning, could be linked to specific areas of the brain. While many aspects of phrenology proved implausible, the basic concept endures today, in the science of **neuropsychology**.

The idea that different behavioral functions related directly to the anatomy of the brain was supported by Paul Broca and Karl Wernicke in the 19th century. They found that different kinds of language impairment occurred after damage to specific areas in the left hemisphere. The notion was further advanced by mapmakers like Wilder Penfield, who mapped the sensory and motor functions of the brain by stimulating the cortex of patients before surgery (1951).

Current understanding of the brain-behavior relationship stems from the notion of **modularity**. This is the idea that all aspects of a given faculty function as a self-contained module (see Topic 1.7). Each module relates to identifiable neural structures in the brain. Rather than being anatomically localized, however, these structures are connected but distributed through the brain—a concept that is supported by evidence from surgery and brain scanning.

While the modules are independent of one another, they also interact with each other, and it is this interaction that influences how we behave.

Scanning reveals increased activity in different areas of the brain when performing different tasks.

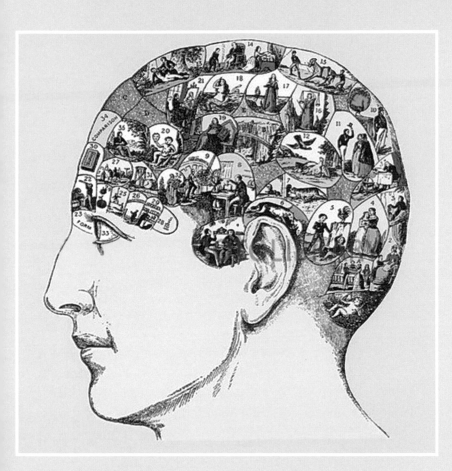

Phrenology was a 19th-century science that argued that different faculties were mirrored in the organization of the brain. Phrenologists correlated character traits with protrusions of the skull to produce maps like the one above, which they then used to ascertain a person's character.

2.2 Brain anatomy

The mammalian brain has evolved from the simpler brains of fish and reptiles. It controls all aspects of behavior.

The brain can be divided into three major components, each comprised of many interconnected structures. They differ in evolutionary age and the complexity of the behaviors they control.

■ **The brainstem**: This is sometimes called the reptilian brain. It controls all basic functions such as eating, drinking, and reproduction. Particularly important, is the reticular activating system. This relays information from the sensory organs to various parts of the brain. It controls consciousness—from sleep through to the heightened arousal found in fighting behavior.

■ **The limbic system and the basal ganglia**: The former is a series of connected structures involved in emotion, memory, and spatial behavior. The latter are a series of structures heavily involved in **motor control** and **associative learning**.

■ **The cerebral cortex**: This layer of cells (gray matter) forms a "cap" on the reptilian brain. It is characterized by extensive folding and is divided into lobes (see opposite). The relative size of the cortex seems related to species intelligence. In mammals it is 80 percent by volume, giving them an evolutionary advantage over other species.

This broad division understates the interconnected nature of the three different structures and the relationship between each of the structures and our behavior.

The human brain consumes about 20 percent of the body's available oxygen. This is hugely disproportionate to its size.

The cortical lobes and their functions

FRONTAL LOBE
Particularly important for
decision-making, motivation/
inhibition, language (selecting
words), and motor control.

PARIETAL LOBE
Particularly important for
calculation, spelling, learned,
skilled gestures, perception,
and body sense/position.

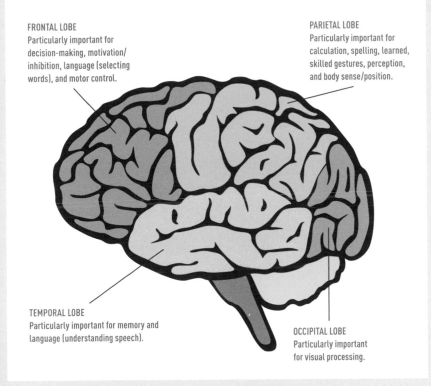

TEMPORAL LOBE
Particularly important for memory and
language (understanding speech).

OCCIPITAL LOBE
Particularly important
for visual processing.

Major folds in the cerebral cortex divide each side of the brain into four
principal lobes: frontal, parietal, temporal, and occipital. Each lobe is
correlated with one or more higher functions.

2.3 The nervous system

The brain is the master controller of a communication network that zaps information around the body.

The nervous system consists of billions of interconnected cells called neurons and it functions as your body's communication network. It is divided in two. The central nervous system (CNS) consists of the brain and spinal cord. The peripheral nervous system (PNS) is a network connecting the CNS to the rest of the body.

In the simplest terms:
- **Afferent neurons** transmit information from the sensory organs (eyes, ears) and the internal organs to the brain.

- **Efferent neurons** transmit operating instructions from the brain to the internal organs and motor organs (hands).

- The brain carries out executive functions, such as interpreting incoming information and decision-making.

The nervous system is further divided into the somatic and autonomic systems. The former controls bodily movements such as walking and talking. The latter controls the internal organs such as the heart, lungs, and stomach.

A third division is of the autonomic system into sympathetic and parasympathetic systems. The sympathetic system is active under conditions that require action, producing increased heart rate, breathing, and a readiness to fight or flee. The parasympathetic system is active in conditions that require normal functioning—eating, resting, sleeping.

Phantom limb is the sensation that a missing limb is still attached. It occurs because the brain area representing the limb is still functioning.

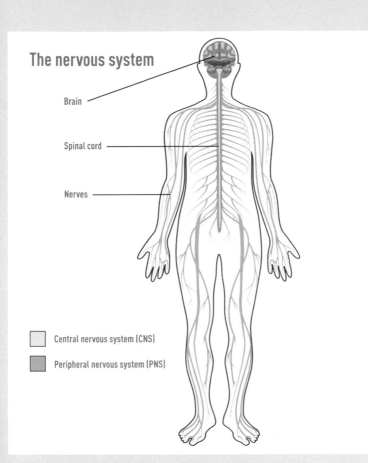

The nervous system

Brain

Spinal cord

Nerves

Central nervous system (CNS)

Peripheral nervous system (PNS)

The CNS consists of the brain and the neural "divided highway," the spinal cord. The PNS consists of "A and B roads" to and from the internal and external structures of the body.

2.4 Neurons and neurotransmitters

A host of electrical and chemical processes take place as information whizzes from one part of the nervous system to the next.

The basic component of the nervous system is the **neuron**. This is a cell consisting of a cell body that receives stimulation from other neurons through its branchlike **dendrites**. It then transmits stimulation to other neurons through a cable-like **axon** (see opposite).

The transmission of information within a neuron is electrical. It receives stimulation from other neurons and when this builds up beyond a given threshold, is activated. It fires, transmitting the stimulation to the next set of neurons. Transmission moves away from the cell body and down the axon, reaching speeds of up to 250 mph (400 kph).

The transmission of information between neurons is chemical. There is a gap between neurons called a synapse. The arrival of a signal at a synapse releases molecules called **neurotransmitters**. These cross the gap and attach to the receiving neuron, thus transmitting the stimulation. More than one type of neurotransmitter can operate at a synapse, and each type communicates with a different subset of neurons.

These electrical and chemical processes occur constantly, allowing neurotransmitters to stimulate specific functions. The neurotransmitter dopamine, for example, is associated with feelings of pleasure and the effectiveness of reward, but also with movement and posture.

Psychotropic drugs, used for treating conditions such as depression, change the way neurotransmitters work.

Neurons and neurotransmitters

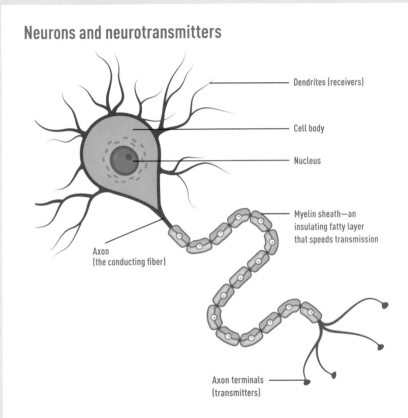

Dendrites (receivers)

Cell body

Nucleus

Myelin sheath—an insulating fatty layer that speeds transmission

Axon (the conducting fiber)

Axon terminals (transmitters)

Stimulation is received by dendrites and transmitted down the axon to other neurons where it is carried across the synapse by neurotransmitters.

2.5 Cell assemblies

How does the brain form and store memories? Evidence suggests that the process starts at a cellular level.

An early question as to whether memories are localized in specific brain cells or distributed over many cells was resolved by the neuropsychologist Donald Hebb (1949). Hebb argued that memories are encoded in **cell assemblies** —connected cells that are distributed across the cortex (see Topic 2.1). These cell assemblies are formed according to the Hebbian rule: Neurons that fire together wire together.

When we learn something, changes occur in the brain at a cellular level—that is within the neurons in the nervous system. Stimulate one neuron with a single, high-frequency, electrical pulse, and activation of the receiving neuron will be enhanced on subsequent occasions (see Topic 2.4). This is called **long-term potentiation**. It shows that a single event can produce a long-term change in the connection between neurons. The effect is stronger with repetition and supports the idea of cell assemblies.

Cell assemblies go some way to explaining how memories are formed and stored. We know that part of the forebrain (the hippocampus) is involved in processing new memories, because amnesics with damage to the hippocampus cannot recall memories from even a few minutes ago. Once processed, new memories are stored in distributed locations across the cortex (see Topic 5.4). We know this because the same amnesics can recall memories from the distant past, when the hippocampus was intact.

The neurosurgeon Wilder Penfield stimulated the cortex of conscious patients to find out which area did what.

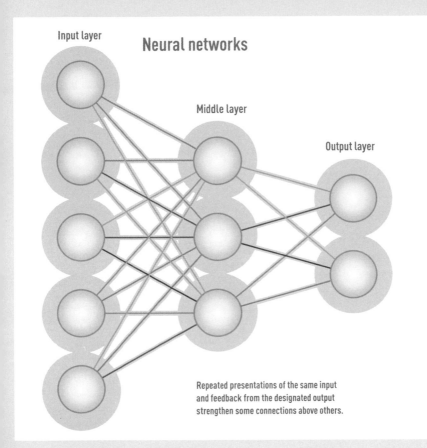

Neural networks

Input layer

Middle layer

Output layer

Repeated presentations of the same input and feedback from the designated output strengthen some connections above others.

Computer simulations have used the Hebbian rule to form associations between a pattern of inputs (say, letters) and a single output (a word). Repeated presentations of the same input and feedback from the designated output strengthen some connections above others.

2.6 The effects of brain damage

By studying the effects of brain damage, scientists are better able to understand the organization of the brain.

Brain damage has different origins and the effects depend on the type of damage caused.

■ A penetrative injury, such as a spike through the skull, can be quite local in its effects.

■ In closed head injuries, such as those that occur in car accidents, violent movement causes the brain to knock suddenly against the skull, causing more **diffuse** damage.

■ The effects of a stroke—when the brain is deprived of blood or when a capillary bursts and floods the brain—depend on how quickly the condition is stopped.

The resulting effects are grouped into sets of loosely connected symptoms called **syndromes**. Damage to memory is amnesia; an inability to recognize objects is agnosia; and lost language functions are known as aphasia.

The often selective nature of damage has contributed hugely to the study of neuropsychology. In particular it has helped to develop the concept of **modularity** (see Topic 2.1). This is the idea that faculties such as visual perception, memory, and language function as independent (but interacting) processes. Conversely, the concept of modularity has advanced our understanding of what often seems to be an assortment of symptoms; for example, the distinction between short- and long-term memory.

Neural stem cells implanted following experimental traumatic brain injury have been found to promote motor and cognitive recovery.

Constructional apraxia

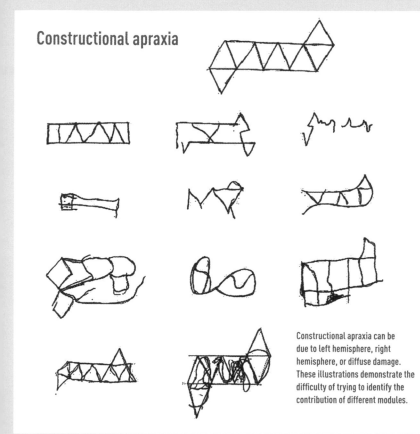

Constructional apraxia can be due to left hemisphere, right hemisphere, or diffuse damage. These illustrations demonstrate the difficulty of trying to identify the contribution of different modules.

Understanding the effects of brain damage is most problematic when it involves multimodule functions such as copying, which include visual perception, visual imagery, planning, and motor control.

2.7 Hormones and behavior

Under certain circumstances and in given situations, our hormones can influence our behavior.

Hormones are slow-acting chemical messengers. Produced by the endocrine glands, they target organs and tissues via the bloodstream. They can influence the way that we behave.

■ **The gonads** produce sex hormones—androgens in males, estrogen and progesterone in females. Female is the default gender, and it is the production of androgens (present in the Y chromosome) that is largely responsible for the development of male sex organs and male gender traits.

■ **Estrogen and progesterone** levels rise during pregnancy and influence maternal behavior after birthing. Major changes in estrogen and progesterone levels occur in a female's lifetime: during menarche (the first period), menstruation, pregnancy, and menopause. These fluctuations may contribute to mood disorders, which are more than twice as frequent in women than they are in men.

■ **The adrenal gland** secretes stress hormones, which are associated with fight or flight reactions to stress. There is clear evidence that male animals are generally more aggressive than females and this is influenced by greater androgen levels prenatally and throughout life.

Immediately following the 1994 World Cup final, in which Brazil defeated Italy, Brazilian spectators were shown to have higher levels of testosterone than Italian fans.

These, and examples like them, go some way to explaining, not only why our behavior patterns vary from person to person, but also between genders.

Aggressive behavior within a species, as demonstrated here by two gemsbok, is usually between males and over resources such as territory and access to females.

2.8 Genes and behavior

It's all in the genes . . . or is it? By studying genetics, scientists try to determine the extent to which our character traits are inherited.

A **gene** is a biological building block. Each one is an instruction to manufacture a kind of cell, and together they function as a recipe to make a particular organism. This recipe—the **genotype**—is composed of genes inherited from each parent when an egg is fertilized by a sperm.

While the genotype is the recipe, the **phenotype** is the resulting trait once the building blocks are assembled. In some cases, it can be traced to a single gene (for example, in dimples and Down syndrome), but most traits arise from the interaction of several genes—eye color and intelligence, for example.

A knotty question is the degree to which a phenotype is inherited or acquired (see Topic 1.10). In order to assess this, scientists study behavior genetics. The key assumption here is that the frequency of a character trait in a given population depends on the degree to which members are genetically related. Siblings, for example, should share more character traits than, say, cousins. Similarly, adopted children ought to resemble their biological parents more closely than their adoptive parents. Identical twins share 50 percent of genes, while fraternal twins share 100 percent.

However, studies have shown that environmental influences play a role too—and the correlations are often complex.

We share some genes with all animals, from 38 percent (roundworm) to 90 percent (chimpanzee).

Genes and schizophrenia

Relationship to individual	Percent of shared genes	Approximate risk	Environment
Identical twin	100%	40–50%	Very similar
Fraternal twin	50%	15–20%	Very similar
Sibling	50%	5–10%	Similar
First cousin	12.5%	0–5%	Variable
General population	0%	1%	Independent

The table represents the risk of being schizophrenic based on the genetic relationship to the affected individual. In cases where the relationship is close, the environment is also likely to be similar. This makes the relative effects of heredity and environment difficult to disentangle.

2.9 Evolution and behavior

Does evolution have a bearing on the ways in which we relate to and respond to our environment?

Evolution is the result of environmental selection over many generations. It occurs because cells mutate and the mutations are then inherited by subsequent generations. Organisms with mutations that aid survival continue to reproduce, while those with mutations that fail to aid survival generally do not.

Evolution adds new structures without removing the old ones. The mammalian brain consists of a basic reptilian brain with added structures such as the cerebral cortex (see Topic 2.2). The older structures are not removed, however, but remain interconnected with newer structures, and may still function. To give an example, people who deny the existence of objects in a portion of the visual field owing to cortical damage (blindsight) continue to show implicit knowledge of these objects because they are using an older visual system.

Who has the longest evolutionary chain? cockroaches: 300 million years; dinosaurs: 135 million years; humanoids: 6 million years.

Darwinists argue that different animals evolve to meet the demands of their specific environment, but that behavioral similarities continue to exist between them. This would explain why the basic fight-or-flight response to threat is found across a huge range of species. **Cartesians**, however, argue that humans represent a behavioral discontinuity in evolutionary terms (see Topic 3.4). They claim that this is best evidenced by the uniqueness of human language.

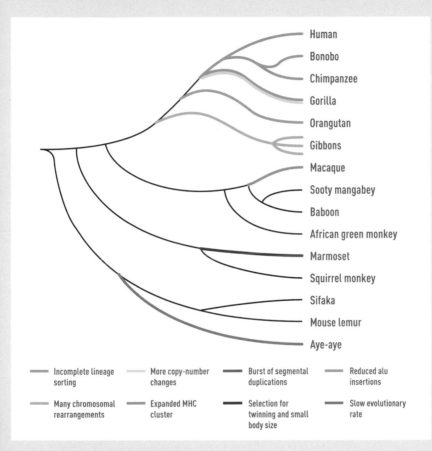

The evolutionary tree shows human lineage in terms of species for which genome sequences are known. (Jeffrey Rogers and Richard A. Gibbs, 2014)

2.10 Comparative psychology

What mechanisms do humans have in common with other species?

Comparative psychology is the study of cross-species behavior to identify both common and species-specific mechanisms. It is anchored in evolutionary theory and offers an opportunity to test hypotheses that may not be testable in humans for ethical or practical reasons.

Consider the powerful social bond between a newborn child and its mother. In many species, this bond forms during a critical period in development. Nobel Laureate Konrad Lorenz showed that just-hatched geese treated the first moving object as their mother, a phenomenon he called imprinting (1935). John Bowlby showed that newborn humans deprived of this maternal bonding developed psychological problems (1951), while Harry Harlow demonstrated that maternally deprived infant monkeys would bond with surrogate mothers consisting of wire effigies covered with toweling (1959).

Skinner elicited superstitious behavior in pigeons (for example, turning in a circle before eating) by delivering food reward arbitrarily.

Another example can be illustrated by the work of behavioral psychologists, led by B. F. Skinner, who worked with rats and pigeons to identify the mechanisms of learning (see also, Topic 6.2). They showed that, while reward promoted long-term learning, punishment only suppressed behavior. While these principles have been applied successfully in educational, clinical, and correctional settings there is a continuing debate as to whether the mechanisms are the same across different species.

Species at different stages of evolutionary development all show tool use, but the sophistication of the tool and its use reflect their physical capabilities, their intellectual ability, and environmental demands.

LIFE-SPAN PSYCHOLOGY

Life-span psychology is also known as developmental psychology. The former term is used more often these days, to reflect the idea that development is not necessarily confined to infancy and childhood: People continue to develop throughout their lives. It is a challenging discipline, which has to consider the interaction of all branches of psychology (cognitive, social, and biological, to name just a few) in order to understand how and why change occurs.

In this chapter, we start by looking at those factors that can influence our development even before we are born. We look at the extent to which the developing brain can compensate for damage during this time. We then explore the structure of the brain and how it processes information. Is the processing of information confined to specific domains or is it more general than that? And does our development

Continues overleaf

have observable milestones or do we simply develop gradually?

We look at infants and the various methods used for testing them. These range from gauging an infant's reaction to a new stimulus to testing his or her ability to process different types of information. What purpose do these tests serve? And how accurate can they be, given that the young cannot articulate their thoughts? There are many aspects of social development and we look at the most important. First there is an infant's understanding of self-recognition. Then we consider theory of mind—the development of an understanding that another person can hold a belief that is different from one's own. A look at friendships sees how they form and the changes they go through over time.

Finally we examine what happens as we age. There is some loss of sensory ability as we get older, but is cognitive decline inevitable?

Contents

3.1 Birth defects

3.2 Brain plasticity

3.3 Structure of the mind

3.4 Continuity and discontinuity

3.5 Testing infants

3.6 Measuring intelligence

3.7 Self-recognition

3.8 Theory of mind

3.9 Forming friendships

3.10 Getting older

3.1 Birth defects

Even before a mother knows she is pregnant, her developing fetus may be exposed to various threats.

There are a number of nongenetic elements—**teratogens**—that can influence embryonic development, causing birth defects. These include ingested substances like alcohol. They can also be environmental—infections like rubella or herpes—or other external factors, such as radiation.

Particular teratogens are associated with specific defects. For example, alcohol is associated with fetal alcohol syndrome, which can result in abnormal growth and/or intellectual difficulties. Radiation can be associated with spina bifida, cleft palate, and blindness, depending on the dosage received. This explains why doctors are very reluctant to x-ray women who may be pregnant.

The timing of exposure to teratogens influences how the embryo is affected, depending upon what is forming at the time. A drug called thalidomide was given to relieve morning sickness in the 1950s and 1960s. It resulted in many infants being born with limb deformities. It was discovered that the time at which the drug was taken determined which limbs were affected and so informed us about critical periods in embryonic development.

Thalidomide is now sometimes used with extreme caution to treat skin lesions caused by leprosy.

Finally, it is not just maternal exposure that can influence fetal development. Some factors also influence sperm. For example, alcohol has been associated with sperm defects leading to low-birth-weight babies.

Teratogens and their effects

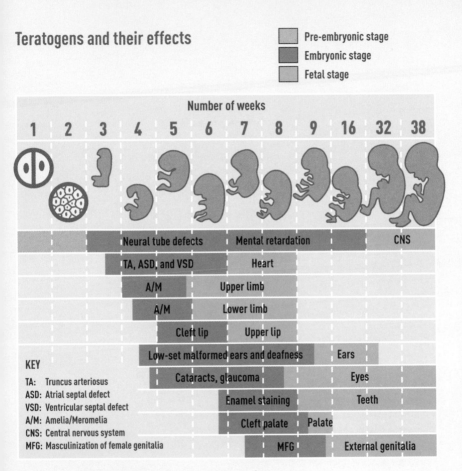

- Pre-embryonic stage
- Embryonic stage
- Fetal stage

KEY

TA: Truncus arteriosus
ASD: Atrial septal defect
VSD: Ventricular septal defect
A/M: Amelia/Meromelia
CNS: Central nervous system
MFG: Masculinization of female genitalia

This table illustrates embryonic and fetal development from conception to birth. It highlights the effects of teratogens at different stages of growth.

3.2 Brain plasticity

The developing brain changes rapidly as it processes information from the outside world, and continues to change throughout life.

The developing brain shows remarkable **plasticity**. This is the ability of the brain's neural pathways to be reorganized by experience. This can result from an infant processing sensory information to make sense of its world, or it can be an adaptive process resulting from brain injury. Reorganization may fall into one of two categories:

- **Experience-expectant reorganization**: This is when the brain is preconfigured by millions of years of evolution to respond to experiences that will shape it further.

- **Experience-dependent reorganization**: This results from specific learning experiences, such as playing the piano or a computer game.

Early developmental psychologists believed that neural networks become stable over time, but more recent evidence suggests that the brain never stops changing. This is the foundation of learning, in which stronger associations are made through experience (see Topic 2.5).

Usually, a hemispherectomy is performed in young children so that the plasticity of the brain results in less damage to cognitive functioning.

Sometimes, in the case of permanent injury, brain plasticity can allow another part of the brain to take over the function of the damaged part of the brain. This is evident from the experiences of brain-injured patients. Occasionally a hemispherectomy is performed in which one hemisphere is removed, usually to alleviate severe seizures.

The adaptable brain

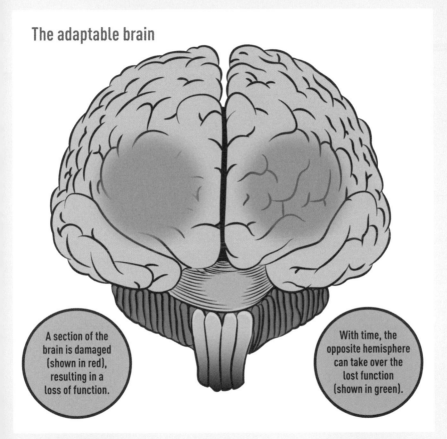

A section of the brain is damaged (shown in red), resulting in a loss of function.

With time, the opposite hemisphere can take over the lost function (shown in green).

An illustration of the plasticity of the brain, where one area of the brain adapts to take over the function of a damaged area of the brain. It does not always have to be symmetrical.

3.3 Structure of the mind

The mind is a complicated entity. At present we can only theorize about its structure.

There is much debate among cognitive developmental psychologists about the structure of the mind in terms of how we think and learn. This can be divided into two distinct areas: **domain generality** and **domain specificity**.

Advocates of domain generality argue that the infant brain develops processes and resources that can be applied independently of context, ready to be shaped by experience. This theory suggests that all reasoning mechanisms are available to all processing.

The contrasting view of domain specificity argues that we are born with innate neural structures that have evolved to perform specific functions. This suggests that mathematical reasoning mechanisms are only available to process information in a mathematical domain, and likewise for other domains. Some researchers argue that this is a pointless debate, since it is impossible to know with any real certainty whether or not there are separate domains.

Fodor's theory of **modularity** of mind (1983) assumes that the mind is domain specific. However, a domain-specific theory does not automatically dictate that the mind is also modular (see Topic 2.1). These theories about the structure of the mind are independent of our understanding of the structure of the brain (see Topic 2.2).

Theories about the structure of the mind are important to scientists trying to develop artificial intelligence.

Domain generality

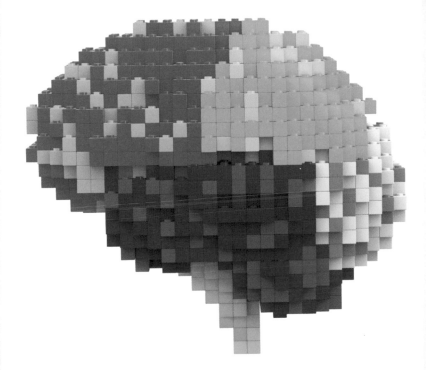

Advocates of domain generality suggest that the mind is analogous with a box of building blocks and that it is our experiences that shape how they are put together.

3.4 Continuity and discontinuity

No one really knows how development happens. What researchers agree on, however, is that it involves a journey that happens over time.

When discussing development, there are two main schools of thought. **Continuity** suggests gradual development that occurs without discernable stages, while **discontinuity** implies development in measureable stages.

A pioneer of discontinuity was Jean Piaget (1896–1980). He suggested that cognitive development happened in the following stages. He stated that each stage must be passed through in this order and that none can be missed out.

- **Sensorimotor stage** (from birth to age two): The use of motor skills to interact with the environment.

- **Preoperational stage** (two to seven years): Reasoning is mainly driven by perception.

- **Concrete operational stage** (seven to twelve years): The emergence of logical thinking but only for real objects.

- **Formal operational stage** (twelve years onward): At this stage, abstract reasoning can be observed.

The philosopher Jean-Jacques Rousseau (1712–1778) discussed human development in terms of stage theory.

Those who believe that development is continuous, cite that infants gradually change over time and not in abrupt stages. They cite that mastery of logical reasoning occurs for some tasks but not others at the same time. For example a child may understand conservation of liquid (that the volume remains the same no matter what shape or size the container) but not transfer that to modeling clay.

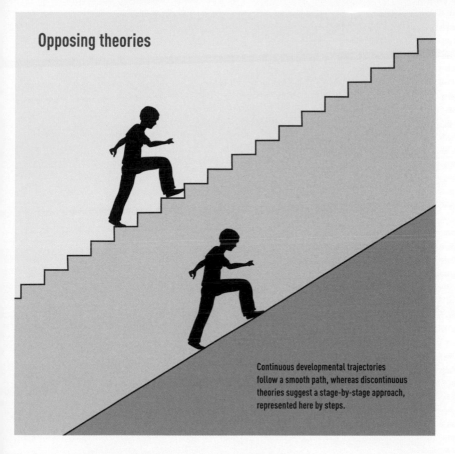

Opposing theories

Continuous developmental trajectories follow a smooth path, whereas discontinuous theories suggest a stage-by-stage approach, represented here by steps.

Developmental trajectories as shown by continuity and discontinuity theory. We start by not being able to do something and end having acquired an ability. But how do we get there?

3.5 Testing infants

Infants have no way of telling us what they are thinking, so how can we make psychological discoveries in children?

There are two methods for testing infants that help us understand sensory and cognitive development: **habituation** and **preferential looking**.

- Habituation is when an infant is repeatedly exposed to a stimulus until it loses interest. This is followed by exposing the infant to a different stimulus. If the new stimulus is perceived as different by the infant, it will take an interest in it. If the new stimulus is perceived as the same, the infant will ignore it. Habituation studies test a range of functions (sound, vision, and so on). They have been used to demonstrate discrimination of small number sets (two and three objects) in three-day-old infants. They have also shown that three-month-olds are surprised when seemingly impossible physical events occur. This suggests some understanding of physical principles.

- Preferential looking shows us that infants process information across a range of interactive functions, such as language, perception, and memory, before they can speak. An example would be an infant sitting on the lap of its caregiver, looking at two screens showing different pictures. A recording plays a phrase such as "Where is the dog?". One screen shows a dog and the other a baby. The infant tends to look at the screen showing the item mentioned, in this case, a dog.

Four-month-old Japanese infants have been known to distinguish between the sounds of the letters "r" and "l," which are not in their native vocabulary.

Preferential looking

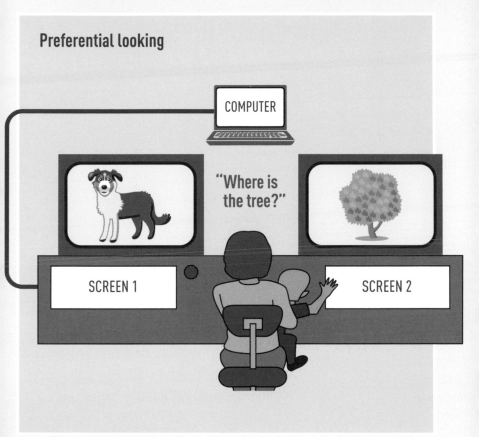

An infant is shown two images and will look at the one corresponding with what he or she hears.

3.6 Measuring intelligence

It is possible to take measurements to assess that mental abilities are developing within the normal range.

When people think of intelligence tests, they often imagine puzzles that tap reasoning ability. Many studies of babies and infants refer to their intelligence, but how do we measure intelligence in those too young to speak or perform complex reasoning tasks?

There are a number of tests available that access cognitive functioning in the very young. Examples of such tests are:

■ The Mullen Scales of Early Learning: Used from birth to 5 years, this tests motor, visual, and language skills.

■ The Bayley Scale of Infant Development: Used from one month to three and a half years, this assesses behavior, motor skills, and mental abilities.

The two main reasons for using these tests are for research purposes, and for those occasions on which a clinician may want to investigate possible developmental delays.

The first intelligence test was the Binet-Simon Intelligence Test published in 1905.

If an infant is not reaching developmental milestones as expected, these assessments can help indicate whether there is a developmental problem, or that the lateness of acquisition is simply down to individual differences (see Topic 8.1). Such research has furthered our understanding of how visual perception and memory skills can be shown to predict intelligence later on.

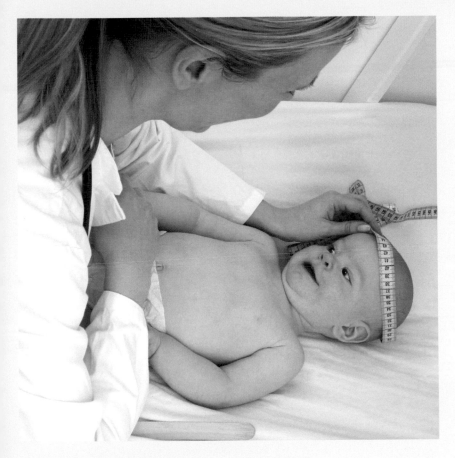

New research from the University of Adelaide shows that weight gain and increased head size in the first month of a baby's life is linked to a higher IQ at early school age.

3.7 Self-recognition

An infant as young as 12 hours old will recognize its mother. But how long is it before an infant knows its own face?

An important milestone in social development is that of self-recognition. This is something an infant cannot do at birth and generally develops around the age of two years.

The rouge removal task uses the assumption that, if an infant recognizes its own face in a mirror and sees an unusual mark on it, it will reach up to remove that mark. Usually a mark is placed surreptitiously on the infant's face by a caregiver. If the infant does not try to remove the mark, the suggestion is the child does not understand that the face it sees in the mirror is its own.

A study looking at self-recognition used video to show children images of themselves playing a game during which a mark is covertly applied to their faces. The study revealed that four- to five-year-olds reached up for the mark after a delay of about three minutes from the activity being shown. One week later they were filmed playing a different game, again with a sticker. This time very few of those same children tried to remove the mark after viewing. This suggests that, by four years, most children can recognize themselves and can use contextual information to compare present state with an earlier state. This is thought to be the emergence of the autobiographical self.

Self-recognition can be observed in some animals such as primates, elephants, dolphins, and magpies, but not in gorillas, gibbons, giant pandas, or African gray parrots.

The rouge removal test

If, during this experiment, the baby recognizes herself, she should reach up and try to remove the mark from her face when shown her reflection in a mirror.

3.8 Theory of mind

How aware are young children of the inner thoughts and reasoning of others?

Social cognition refers to an area of psychology in which we try to understand social behavior by investigating the cognitive processes behind it. A fundamental part of this is an understanding of what other people may be thinking or what they believe. The term theory of mind is used to describe this ability and marks an important milestone in a child's development.

The ability is often tested using a false-belief test. A child will be shown a scenario in which it knows something is false, while another person believes it to be true. A classic example of this is the Sally–Anne task:

• The child observes Sally and Anne together, putting a marble in a basket.

• Sally leaves the scene and Anne moves the marble to another location.

• The child is asked "where will Sally look for the marble?"

• If the child has developed a theory of mind, it will answer "in the basket" because, although the child knows that the marble has been moved, it also knows that Sally is unaware of this and will go to where she had left it.

Children generally pass the false-belief test by about four years of age. However, those with autism have trouble passing this test even when much older.

The term theory of mind was first used in a research paper about chimpanzees and was only used to refer to human social cognition later on.

The Sally–Anne task

This is Sally.

Sally has a basket.

This is Anne.

Anne has a box.

Sally has a marble. She puts the marble into her basket.

Sally goes out for a walk.

Anne takes the marble out of the basket and puts it in the box.

Now Sally comes back. She wants to play with her marble.

Where will Sally look for her marble?

The Sally–Anne task is a classic example of a false-belief test.
The ability to understand the mental states of others is an important
skill when it comes to social interaction.

3.9 Forming friendships

From birth, right through the teen years, a child's friendships are based on a diverse range of criteria that change as a child grows older.

Young infants have opportunity friends. These are usually the children of their parents' friends. Once a child is in a wider social setting, such as a playgroup or school, it has greater opportunity for forming friendships among its own peers and can influence who those friends are.

At around the age of seven to eight years, friendships are formed for convenience, with those who live nearby or have the best toys. At around ten years, children start to develop friendships with others who share their values—for example, liking similar games. By around 13 years, the most important factor is a mutual understanding of each other.

Peer interactions can involve either conversation or physical play. Even in young children, play between friends is more complex than play between non-friends. When there is dispute, friends are more likely to try to resolve it, while non-friends are happy to just walk away.

When young, disputes and aggression are more likely to center around a play object or game rules and be physical. Children of mid-childhood age (around 12 years) are more likely to replace physical aggression with direct insults. At this stage, many children focus on what activities other children engage in, using this to build social maps to decide if others are friends or enemies.

Reputational salience is the term given to those things that contribute to a child's social reputation within a peer group.

Friendships from birth

mutual likes

school

family friends

play group

community connections

family

best toys

neighbors

PRESCHOOL

shared values

7 TO 12 YEARS

12 YEARS +

KEY

Opportunity

Convenience

Mutual understanding

Young children make friendships from birth onward. The nature of those friendships—the types of friends made and the activities shared—change as a child grows older.

3.10 Getting older

Aging comes to us all and, with it, a host of inevitable biological changes. What is the impact of this on our brains?

Changes that happen as we get older are different than those that occur in childhood. Studies have shown deficits in sensory and perceptual abilities (hearing, sight, mobility), which can influence social interaction and therefore have an effect on psychological well-being.

Some cognitive functions are less susceptible to change over time than others. Attention can decline with age, particularly selective attention. This slows, making it harder to attend to one specific thing when several things are going on. The ability to divide attention also declines, making it harder to attend to more than one thing at a time.

Intelligence can be described as being fluid or crystallized. The former involves the ability to reason logically about a problem. The latter is the result of experience and gained knowledge. As we age, our crystallized intelligence increases, because we have gained more experience. However, fluid intelligence seems to decrease with age. This makes it harder to reason in unfamiliar settings and gives the impression that older people are confused when they simply need more time to process information.

A chess player showed no sign of dementia when alive. When he died, his brain showed all the signs of advanced Alzheimer's, suggesting we can ward off cognitive decline.

There are other reasons older people may have difficulties with certain tasks. Brain changes can result in dementia. This results in deterioration in all mental faculties, yet it often starts with memory deficits (see Topic 9.5).

Ages and stages

1: Baby—learning to crawl.
2: Toddler—onset of language.
3: Schoolchild—developing social skills.
4: Emerging adulthood—gaining independence.
5: Parenthood—responsibility to family.
6: Middle age—dealing with midlife stress.
7: Onset of seniority—start of sensory losses.
8: Seniority—potential degenerative disease.

Our development starts from before birth and continues from the
cradle to the grave. With each milestone we may face a new set of
skills to learn or age-related health issues.

SOCIAL BEHAVIOR

4

Many psychologists would argue that all psychology is social psychology and that very little of our existence is truly independent of those around us. This chapter focuses on the idea that the way we think, feel, and behave is affected—either directly or indirectly—by the social beings and structures around us.

Over the following pages, we examine a number of subdisciplines within the area of social psychology. Some, such as forming attitudes and stereotypes, are to do with the way we think about things and people. How do these thoughts form and how can they be changed? We also explore our need to find rational explanations for the actions and words of others—for only then can we make sense of the world around us.

Digging deeper, we take a look at the influences that other people can have on our own behavior. In doing so, we

Continues overleaf

attempt to understand why we choose to help other people sometimes, but not others. This leads us into the realms of conformity and obedience—areas that often see us behaving in a manner that we might least expect.

We look at the ways in which others around us can either increase or decrease our productivity and performance—this centers on the related phenomena of social facilitation and loafing. Finally, we introduce the perspective of social identity, which highlights how our selves are intimately tied up in the various groups to which we belong.

What all these areas share is the concept of social influence—the idea that, in some sense, the way we think, feel, and behave routinely depends on the behavior of those around us.

Contents

4.1 Forming attitudes

4.2 Forming impressions

4.3 Forming stereotypes

4.4 Susceptibility to persuasion

4.5 Making attributions

4.6 Helping bystanders

4.7 Conforming to others

4.8 Acts of obedience

4.9 Social facilitation and loafing

4.10 Social identity

4.1 Forming attitudes

We constantly make judgments about objects, ideas, and entities in our social world. But how do they take shape?

Psychologist Daniel Katz (1903–98) argued that we display a number of characteristics when forming attitudes. These include:

- A need to make sense of the world.

- A need to obtain rewards and avoid punishments (by holding socially acceptable opinions).

- A desire to express strong convictions.

- A need to defend ourselves from psychological threats (by having positive attitudes toward ourselves).

Forming an attitude can involve one or more of these factors. The more complex an attitude is, the more extreme it can become.

Studies show that attitudes can be held implicitly as well as explicitly—that is, we form them without an awareness of doing so (see Topic 6.5). As such, they are quick to form but slow to change. They affect spontaneous, unplanned behavior.

In contrast, explicit attitudes, also influenced by evidence and reflection, take more input to form but can change quickly. They are often influenced by social norms and planned behaviors. These trends suggest that we seek balance in our attitudes.

Some attitudes, such as general political conservatism, may have a genetic basis.

Balance theory

If I like a person but dislike the object, and that person likes the object, the triad is unbalanced.

By changing the value of one of the lines I can achieve balance.

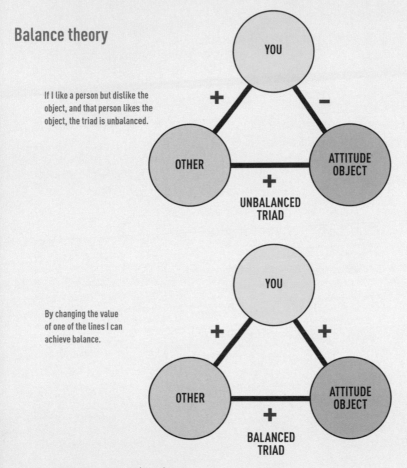

YOU

+ −

OTHER + ATTITUDE OBJECT

UNBALANCED TRIAD

YOU

+ +

OTHER + ATTITUDE OBJECT

BALANCED TRIAD

Fritz Heider's balance theory (1958) demonstrates that we seek balance between our attitudes toward a person, an object, and the person's attitude to that object.

4.2 Forming impressions

Thirty to sixty seconds is all it takes for us to make judgments about the people we encounter.

We judge the personalities of others all the time, but how do we form impressions, and how good at it are we?

Researchers such as Solomon Asch suggest that our decisions about others revolve around certain fundamental traits (1946). Our evaluation of these traits colors our evaluation of other attributes. For example, seeing someone as being a warm or cold person can influence how likable or reliable we perceive them, and so on. These evaluations may be automatic.

Other models of impression formation, such as Norman Anderson's cognitive algebraic models (1962), suggest that we combine our evaluations of positive and negative traits to make one overall judgment (see opposite). We generally place more emphasis on negative than positive traits.

First impressions, in particular, influence our judgments, and are very hard to alter once established. Dana Carney and colleagues suggest we are actually reasonably good at evaluating some traits, including extroversion, intelligence, and conscientiousness very quickly (2007).

Along with physical appearance, facial expression, and other information, we also use the attributions of others' behaviors and our stereotypes around their group membership(s) when forming impressions (see Topics 4.2 and 4.5).

When forming impressions, we generally place greater emphasis on negative than positive traits.

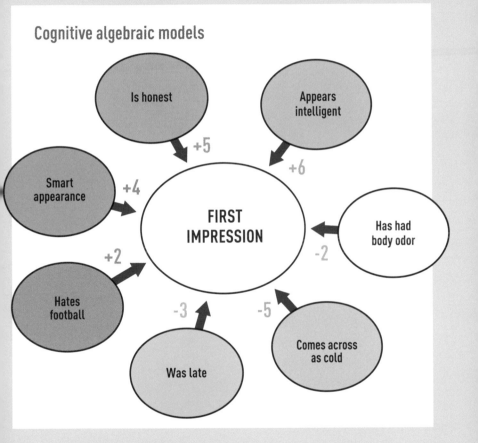

Cognitive algebraic models

Is honest +5

Appears intelligent +6

Smart appearance +4

FIRST IMPRESSION

Has had body odor -2

Hates football +2

Was late -3

Comes across as cold -5

Models like the one above involve making judgments of various positive and negative dimensions, each of which has a different weighting on the final decision. In this example, the person scores +7—a positive first impression.

4.3 Forming stereotypes

Categorizing people into types rather than viewing them as individuals helps us to make sense of the world, but it has a downside.

When forming stereotypes, we tend to make judgments of others based on their membership to a particular group, ignoring or minimizing any personal differences. The Stereotype Content model (2002) suggests that stereotypes contain judgments based on how much warmth or competence we perceive a person or group to have. Different combinations lead to different responses:

- Groups that some may perceive as high warmth, low competence—say, mothers—elicit active behaviors and patronizing feelings.

- Low warmth, high competence groups (nationalities seen as competent but disdainful) elicit feelings such as jealousy and attract hostile behaviors.

- Low competence, low warmth groups (perhaps homeless people) attract avoidance and pity or disgust.

- High warmth, high competence groups attract facilitative behaviors and emotions including admiration.

We frequently form stereotypes subconsciously, searching out stereotype-consistent evidence, while ignore stereotype-inconsistent information. This makes stereotypes resistant to change. Indeed, we are more prone to create a subgroup of individuals within a category than to change our stereotype of the group as a whole.

> Stereotypes can affect our behavior toward others. This affects their responses, so creating a vicious cycle.

Gender stereotypes

Chatting at a party, George and Cindy are equally matched in height. The next day, George recalls Cindy being shorter than him. This is down to gender stereotyping.

Research shows that people often guess the heights of others erroneously owing to gender stereotypes. The effects of stereotypes on basic cognitive processes are one reason they are hard to change.

4.4 Susceptibility to persuasion

Can you be persuasive? Success has as much to do with the mood of your audience as the compelling delivery of your message.

Persuasion is an enormous topic in psychology. Here, discussion is based on three models: the Yale model; the heuristic-systematic model (HSM); and the elaboration likelihood model (ELM).

■ **The Yale model** argues that the source of a message, the message itself, and its recipient are all important factors. To be persuasive, therefore, the source should be attractive, likable, credible, and similar to the recipient. Short, strong messages are more influential than long weak ones. They should be consistent and repeated often.

■ **The HSM** argues that we process messages in one of two ways. The first is systematic. We focus on the substance of an argument, its logic, and veracity. The second is peripheral, and relies more on **heuristics**—what is the source of the message, how long is it?

■ **The ELM** argues that, when motivated, able, and attentive, a recipient processes messages in considerable depth (high elaboration). When lacking in motivation or distracted, he or she doesn't (low elaboration).

While systematic and high-elaboration processing require greater effort to achieve an attitudinal change, that change is nevertheless more stable and longer-lasting.

Some evidence suggests that women and young adults are more susceptible to persuasion than men and older adults.

Elaboration likelihood model

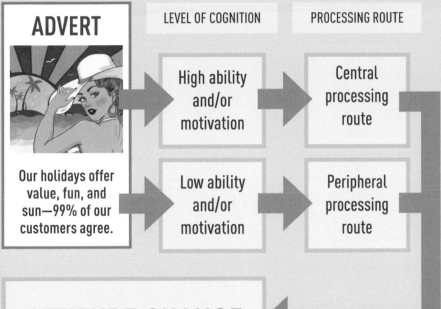

The ELM argues that, when confronted with advertising, we can take central or peripheral routes of processing. Each route is affected by different cues and leads to different types of change.

4.5 Making attributions

Certain biases come into play when we try to interpret, not only the behavior of others, but also of ourselves.

When we try to explain why other people behave the way they do, the attributions we make fall into two major categories. They are either internal—that is, to do with an individual's personality. Or they are external and relate to an individual's situation.

In his covariation models of 1973, Harold Kelley suggested that our judgments are driven, in part, by how consistent an individual's behavior is. Firstly, how consistent is the behavior in relation to that of other people? Secondly, how consistent is the behavior in relation to your experience of that individual at other times and in other situations?

It is interesting to note that, when making attributions about other people, we tend to view their behavior in terms of personality, particularly if they behave in socially undesirable ways. We tend to view our own behavior as driven more by the situations in which we find ourselves.

There is also evidence to suggest that biases are culturally specific. For example, a young child in a collectivist society (India) will make the same proportion of external and internal attributions as a child in an individualistic society (America). However, as the children age, they develop biases—collectivist cultures toward external attributions and individualistic cultures toward internal (see Topic 8.8).

Observing your own behavior in a mirror leads to you attributing it more to situational influences!

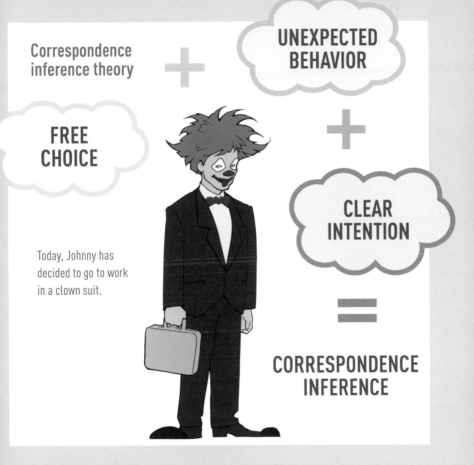

Correspondence inference theory **+** UNEXPECTED BEHAVIOR

FREE CHOICE

+

CLEAR INTENTION

Today, Johnny has decided to go to work in a clown suit.

=

CORRESPONDENCE INFERENCE

Jones and Davis's correspondence inference theory suggests that behavior reflects a person's traits when all three attributes—free choice, unexpected behavior, and clear intention—are present.

4.6 Helping bystanders

People are capable of acts of heroism in emergency situations, but they can also fail to intervene. Why?

Psychologists use models of helping behavior to explain the motivation behind bystander helping.

Essentially, when encountering an emergency, we need to decide whether or not to take responsibility—that is, to become involved. Once committed we select a helping behavior and act upon it. But what motivates us to take responsibility in the first place?

Piliavin and colleagues offer a solution in their cost-reward model of 1969. They suggest that viewing a victim in an emergency situation generates negative psychological arousal, which we are motivated to reduce.

Initially we appraise factors that enable helping behaviors along the following lines: What is the reward for doing so? Will I be censored by others if I don't help, and so on. We also appraise factors that inhibit our aid, such as the likely risks involved. In weighing up these enablers and inhibitors, we decide whether to help directly or indirectly, whether to ignore the situation, or to reframe how we perceive it. Helping may also be affected by the extent we view the victim's predicament to be of his or her own doing (see Topic 4.5).

The more people that witness an emergency, the less likelihood there is of an individual helping. This is referred to as bystander apathy.

Responding to an accident

In emergency situations where the need to help is clear and people
know how to respond, assistance is much more likely. Training can
help with both of these factors and increase intervention rates.

4.7 Conforming to others

We consistently match our thoughts, attitudes, and/or behaviors to those around us. We do so even despite our misgivings.

Conformity causes changes in our behavior and happens as a result of social influence (see Topics 4.4 and 4.8).

Muzafer Sherif was the first to demonstrate the tendency to conform in his experiment of 1936. He asked participants to estimate how much a pin-point of light in a darkened room was moving. In reality, the light was stationary, any movement being the result of an optical effect. Even without any frame of reference, when participants performed this experiment as a group, their estimates converged after only a few trials.

Solomon Asch's experiments of 1951 achieved similar results. He showed that, when presented with a set of comparator lines and a standard line (see opposite), people are highly accurate at matching the standard to the right comparator. However, on hearing a number of other participants—in this case, stooges—name a different line, it was not uncommon for a participant also to name the erroneous line. Surprisingly, only 25% of participants never conformed at all.

In Asch's studies, 50 percent of participants conformed to erroneous judgments at least half of the time.

These two series of studies started a large program of research that explores when and how people conform to others.

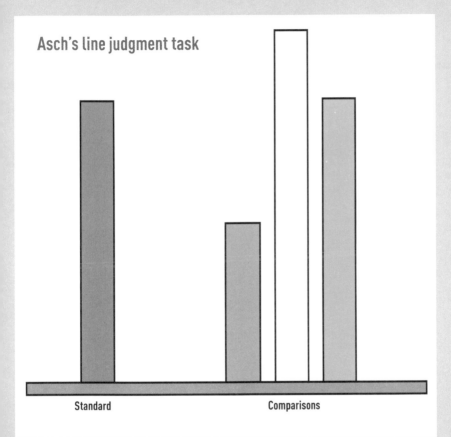

Asch's line judgment task

Standard   Comparisons

This is, perhaps, the most famous set of lines in psychology.
Asch showed that people will conform to the judgments of others
(publically at least), even when it defies the evidence before them.

4.8 Acts of obedience

Could you pump a stranger with 450 volts of electricity? Think again. Sometimes the urge to obey makes us do curious things.

During the 1960s, the Milgram studies produced the most startling results when observing the characteristics of obedience. In this series of experiments, individuals administered electric shocks of increasing intensity to someone they believed to be a fellow participant with a minor heart condition.

As the supposed shocks intensified from 15 to 450 volts, the fellow participant—actually an actor—was heard to scream and whimper in another room. Should an individual hesitate in giving a shock, he or she was told by the experimenter—the authority in this study—that they had to continue, or the experiment would be a failure.

Prior to the study, Stanley Milgram surveyed a number of experts and nonexperts to ask them what proportion of people would deliver what level of shock. Most predicted that no participants would deliver over 300 volts. Experts suggested only ten percent would exceed 180 volts with only 0.01 percent reaching the maximum. The reality? Some 20 percent delivered shocks greater than 150 volts; 63 percent of them gave a potentially lethal 450-volt shock.

Despite the ethical issues around this research—and society has changed since the 1960s—this is a powerful demonstration of the effects of authority, and how normal people can do terrible things in some contexts.

Seeing the participant, or having the individuals wear masks, altered levels of compliance in the Milgram studies.

Obeying the rules

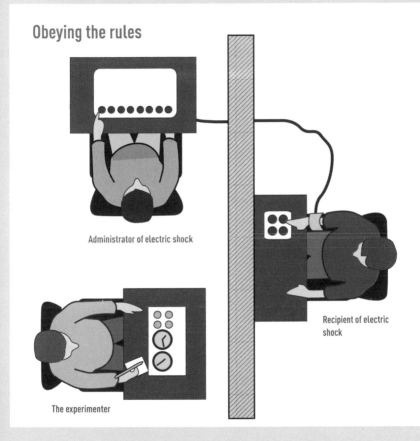

Administrator of electric shock

Recipient of electric shock

The experimenter

The subjects of this experiment could not see the recipient. They could only hear the screams. Despite obvious physical pain, this did not stop the majority of them from administering electric shocks.

4.9 Social facilitation and loafing

Why is it that the presence of others can influence the way that we perform?

Social facilitation is the phenomenon of increased performance caused by the presence of others. It was first observed by Norman Triplett in 1898, who witnessed cyclists racing faster against pace bikes.

In 1965, Robert Zajonc argued that the presence of others facilitated performance of simple tasks, but inhibits performance of complex or new, unpracticed ones. There could be several reasons for these effects. The performer may feel apprehensive about being judged, for example, or may simply be distracted.

Social loafing occurs when a group of people produces less collective effort than one would expect from the sum of the individuals' abilities. Numerous tasks have been studied, including laughing, being creative, and physical sports. The phenomenon seems to result from a lack of team coordination and a loss of motivation.

The effects of social loafing are strongest when individuals are unaccountable for their performance, suspect others will underperform, or are free-riding on the efforts of others. Typically, as group size increases, so too does the discrepancy.

Research into facilitation and loafing ranks among the earliest empirical social psychological investigations.

One way or another, the two phenomena can have a significant impact on your performance in a given situation.

Pulling your weight

If each person can pull four units of force when alone, the total pulling power of a four-person group should be sixteen units. If the total is less than this, then social loafing is occurring.

4.10 Social identity

Belonging to a group allows us to feel good about ourselves, sometimes at the expense of others.

Developed by Henri Tajfel and John Turner (1979) social identity theory argues that belonging to a group benefits us psychologically. It could be a religious group, a footballers' fan club, or whatever. The reason for this is that group membership allows us to make favorable comparisons between our **ingroup** and other **outgroups**.

John Turner and colleagues' self-categorization theory (1987) suggests that sometimes we see ourselves as individuals, sometimes as group members, and sometimes as a mix of the two. In any given situation, we will select the identity that maximizes our ability to compare our group favorably with other groups.

When a group identity is selected, we see the world from the group's perspective and treat other people as group members instead of individuals (see Topic 4.3). We display characteristics and experience emotional reactions that are typical to our group (see opposite).

We tend to see ingroup members as being more varied and outgroup members as less varied than they are. These group level effects can occur even if we are placed in arbitrary groups with little or no history.

Much of our self-identity is based on the social memberships we hold. They can affect the ways in which we think and behave, particularly toward others.

We have many social identities. The ones that come to the fore in a given situation depend on the context.

Self-identity

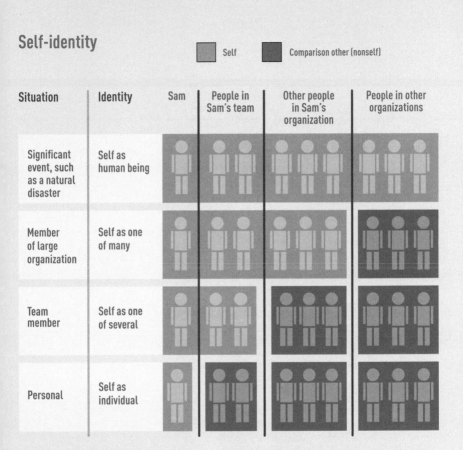

| | Self | | Comparison other (nonself) |

Situation	Identity	Sam	People in Sam's team	Other people in Sam's organization	People in other organizations
Significant event, such as a natural disaster	Self as human being				
Member of large organization	Self as one of many				
Team member	Self as one of several				
Personal	Self as individual				

Self-identity varies depending on the situation. At times of large-scale crisis, Sam may identify with all humans. At work, he may see himself as a team member or a representative of his organization at a multi-company event. On a personal level, he'll see himself as an individual.

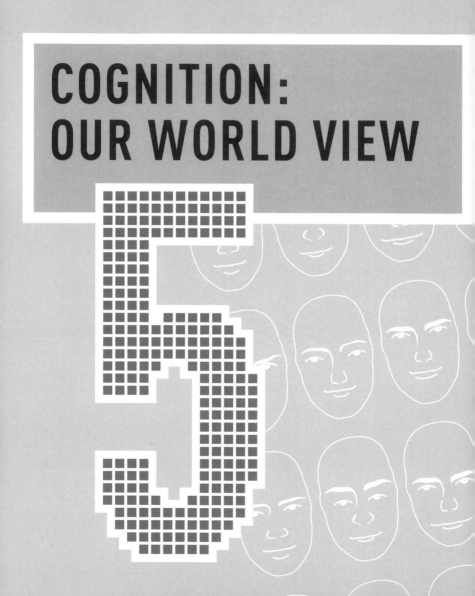

COGNITION: OUR WORLD VIEW

5

Cognition is a term applied to a number of complex mental processes which, together, enable us to understand and interact with the world around us. Cognitive psychology examines how these processes work and interact.

The chapter begins with a look at perception—the brain's window on the world. Just how do we produce a three-dimensional image of the world from patterns of light on the retina?

The next three topics concern memory, specifically object and face recognition; the brain's complex memory systems; and various memory processes. We reveal how memories are encoded as mental representations, consolidated for storage, and then retrieved when required.

Subsequent topics consider the ways in which we carry out complex tasks. How

Continues overleaf

does the brain coordinate the various stages of, say, a grocery shopping trip. There are various modular processes involved here, and they need to work together in order to complete the task. This is where a supervisory process called executive function comes into play. This ties in with our ability not only to focus our attention on specific things, but also to divide our attention between competing tasks when required to do so.

Our brains are capable of wide-ranging mental activities. First, we have a workspace—working memory—devoted almost entirely to problem solving. Then, of course, there are our unique language skills. Both are discussed in detail.

The final two sections of this chapter demonstrate how judgments and choices are made using rules of thumb rather than statistical reasoning. We consider how our reasoning skills are heavily influenced by real world knowledge as well as logic. Food for thought!

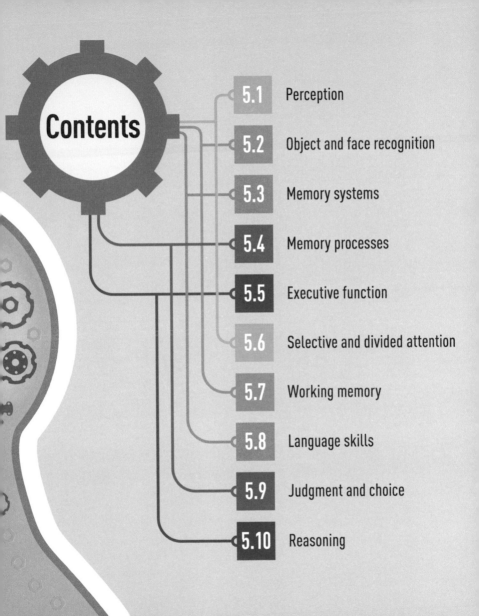

Contents

5.1 Perception

5.2 Object and face recognition

5.3 Memory systems

5.4 Memory processes

5.5 Executive function

5.6 Selective and divided attention

5.7 Working memory

5.8 Language skills

5.9 Judgment and choice

5.10 Reasoning

5.1 Perception

Our senses are like windows on the world. The brain processes the information it receives to allow us to recognize and navigate the world around us.

We receive information from sight, sound, smell, taste, touch, and body position. This information is processed rapidly and without awareness, to produce a mental representation, or **percept**, of the world around us at that point in time. The focus here is on visual perception.

How do we derive a three-dimensional percept from a two-dimensional pattern on the retina? An early stage is identifying an object's features—a table's corners, horizontal edges, vertical edges, and so on activate different cells in the brain. Nobel Laureates David Hubel and Torsten Wiesel found physiological evidence for this. These features are then reassembled using **Gestalt** principles such as proximity. This is the idea that features that are close together probably belong to the same object. The three-dimensional nature of the object is derived from cues such as perspective (think converging railway lines) and the angular disparity between the images reaching each eye.

In order to use this visual information to navigate the world, we need information about the size, shape, and location of objects. We also need constant feedback about how this information changes with movement. Neuropsychological research has identified two relevant cortical pathways that process this information: a what is it pathway and a where is it pathway.

Brain-injured people with blindsight deny seeing an object, but act as if they can see it.

Visual illusions

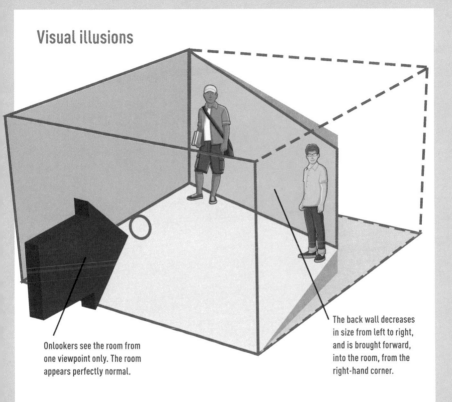

Onlookers see the room from one viewpoint only. The room appears perfectly normal.

The back wall decreases in size from left to right, and is brought forward, into the room, from the right-hand corner.

In the Ames Room, the cues to perception of depth are manipulated to produce an illusion. Although the two boys are the same height, one appears to be a giant compared to the other.

5.2 Object and face recognition

Recognition involves comparing an image to those in a memory bank until a match is found. Experience and expectation both have a role to play.

Using evidence from physiology and experimental psychology the computer scientist David Marr produced a highly influential computer model of the psychological processes thought to underpin visual object recognition (1982). It begins with a representation of an object as a mosaic of brightness pixels (simulating the retina, see also Topic 5.1). Next, features, such as edges and corners, are extracted and bound together. Finally, the model derives a three-dimensional representation of the percept. A memory bank is then searched until a match is found.

Marr's model explains the recognition of man-made objects to a significant degree, but is problematic when it comes to face recognition. Because all faces have the same features (nose, mouth, and so on), recognition depends more on the configuration of features and on characteristics such as skin texture, the depth of the face, and its outline shape and hairline.

Some kinds of head injuries render an individual incapable of recognizing familiar faces— even those of their spouses, children, and parents.

So how do we recognize objects and faces from different points of view, when partly hidden and in generally difficult conditions? To some extent we rely on a limited ability to mentally rotate the percept to an angle that optimizes recognition. We also have a memory bank of the object or face seen previously from different points of view and in different conditions. Finally, we have the power of expectation simply to make an intelligent guess.

Configural processing

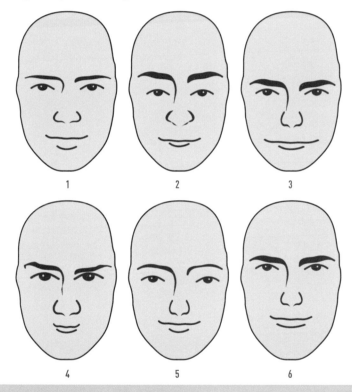

1   2   3

4   5   6

Take any face from the above group, write a detailed description of it, pass the book and your description to a friend, and ask him/her to state which face you are describing. This is surprisingly difficult.

5.3 Memory systems

Knowing how to fly a kite relies on one memory system, while your knowledge of European capital cities relies on another.

Our memories are diverse. We have memories for both recent events and remote ones, for sights and sounds, for facts and figures, events and skills, and so on. Such diversity suggests a complex system (see opposite).

A major distinction is between short-term and long-term memory. The former holds information for only a few seconds, while the latter can retain content for many years. Long-term memory has been divided further into declarative and nondeclarative memory systems.

Declarative memory is for events and facts. It requires active remembering (for example, the events on your last birthday). This system may be divided further into episodic memory (events) and semantic memory (facts).

Nondeclarative memory consists of three subsystems, each of which relates to a different kind of learning. Here, the products of learning are demonstrated by reproducing what was learnt, rather than actively recalling data. We demonstrate knowing how to ride a bike by doing it, not by describing what we learnt.

People with amnesic syndrome can learn new skills but are unable to remember anything about the learning episodes.

Prospective memory is the power to remember to do things in the future. It requires both the declarative and nondeclarative memory systems as well as executive functions such as planning (see Topic 5.5).

Long-term memory

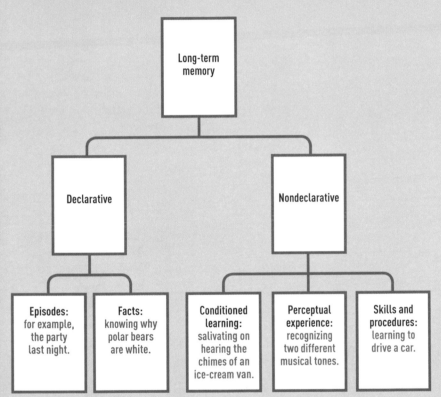

Memory consists of an alliance of systems. Some of the major systems of long-term memory are depicted above, along with examples of the kinds of activities they involve.

5.4 Memory processes

We seem able to recall information on one occasion, but not on another. Are we poorly served by our memory?

Memory depends on the detail with which information is **encoded**, the degree to which it is **consolidated**, and the efficiency with which it is found and **retrieved**. How this happens depends on the types of memories we have.

Events happen in the context of a time, a place, and so on. The memory trace of an event is encoded with this context and tied to existing memories. Memories of facts are tied to related factual memories.

Consolidation of a memory trace can be synaptic or systemic. Synaptic consolidation is temporary and is associated with short-term memory. Systemic consolidation is the mechanism for long-term storage. Memories are processed in the brain by the **hippocampus** and stored remotely, in distributed locations across the cortex.

Remembering is an active process of search and retrieval. It is dependent on cues provided by the situation, for example, questions like "Where were you last evening?" This dependency often makes retrieval unreliable. The process also sees memories elaborated through inference and extrapolation, which makes it susceptible to distortion. When our memory fails, it is usually down to poor encoding, poor consolidation, because similar memories become confounded, or because the retrieval cues are insufficient. In spite of these many points of weakness our ability to recall memories from previous decades is truly remarkable.

A psychologist was once mistakenly accused of rape because the victim happened to see his face on television during the attack. (Baddeley et al, 2009)

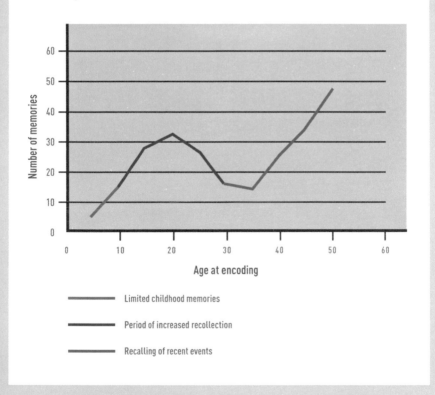

Memory recall

Number of memories (y-axis)
Age at encoding (x-axis)

— Limited childhood memories

— Period of increased recollection

— Recalling of recent events

This idealized graph plots the number of memories that can be retrieved from different points in the life span. While early memories are few, those from young adulthood are plentiful. From about the age of 40, remembering increasingly becomes a question of how recent the event was.

5.5 Executive function

Each of us relies on a dedicated number of processes which, acting together, prioritize and coordinate conscious mental activity.

A seminal paper by Donald Norman and Tim Shallice (1980) argued that two systems govern our everyday lives.

The first is **automated** and drives everyday, highly repetitive behaviors such as going to work. These processes are actually complex tasks, but are so heavily overlearned that we carry them out without thinking.

The second system is an **executive** system that is required for all other complex tasks. So going shopping requires goal setting (a list), planning and prioritizing the stages involved (which shops in what order?), and coordinating perception, memory, and action (where are you, where have you been, where next?). Together, these processes serve an **executive function**. Identifying those processes more precisely, we learn that shopping requires the sequencing of actions and the switching of attention between the different parts of the task. Successful completion depends on focusing on the task in hand and inhibiting distractions. It is difficult to explain how all of this works without invoking a homunculus or "little person in the head."

A patient with environmental dependency syndrome resulting from frontal lobe damage will imitate everything a therapist does, to the minutest detail.

The importance of executive functioning is seen after damage to the frontal lobes of the brain. In such cases, people may show few impairments to intelligence, language, perception, or memory, yet their lives can fall apart because they become distractible and unable to coordinate everyday activities.

The little person in your head

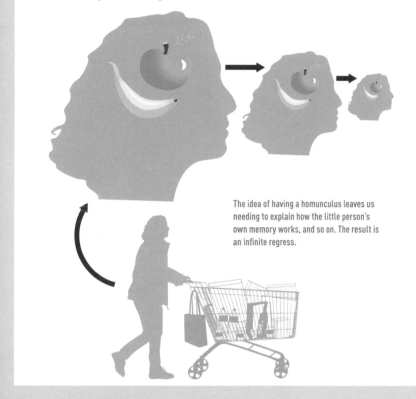

The idea of having a homunculus leaves us needing to explain how the little person's own memory works, and so on. The result is an infinite regress.

Explaining how executive function actually works is difficult without invoking a supervisory mechanism.

5.6 Selective and divided attention

Some tasks demand our full attention, while others require us to divide our attention.

Selective auditory attention is the ability to listen to one message while ignoring others. Donald Broadbent (1958) explained this in terms of an **auditory channel** that can process a single message, while filtering out unwanted messages. To explain why some messages get through —for example, when someone calls your name—there is a rapid switching mechanism that samples unattended messages from time to time.

Selective visual attention has been characterized by Michael Posner as a spotlight that directs attention toward a selected target. This is done covertly (inside the head) but is reflected in overt shifts in gaze. Like a spotlight, the attentional beam can be shifted between targets and focused to a point or spread more widely. Unlike a spotlight it can be divided between two spatially separate targets.

When attention has to be divided between simultaneous tasks, performance tends to deteriorate in comparison to focusing on one task. However, extensive practice can automatize the processes involved to reduce attentional demands. Nevertheless there are limits as to what can be achieved. For example, two actions can be carried out at the same time, but two decisions can't be made simultaneously.

An experiment by Spelke et al (1976) showed that two students were able, after thousands of trials, to read for meaning and write to dictation simultaneously.

There is no doubt that both selective and divided attention are important skills when carrying out complex tasks.

Broadbent's auditory filter model

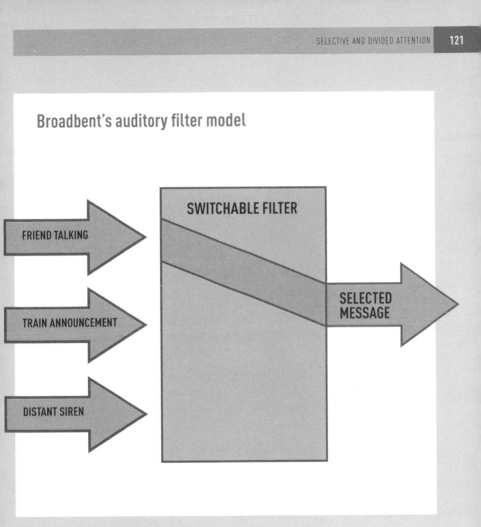

When there are several auditory messages, one is selected and passed on for further processing. The others are excluded but are sampled frequently in case they contain important information.

5.7 Working memory

We all have a mental workspace dedicated to things like mental arithmetic and problem solving. The bigger this is, the better.

Attempts have been made to identify the structure of working memory, and to assess the relationship between working-memory capacity and performance.

Alan Baddeley and Graham Hitch argued that working memory consists of a **central executive**—a director of operations, if you like (1974). Its role is to allocate attention, prioritize, and coordinate. It is served by two slave systems:

■ The **phonological loop** holds and refreshes verbal information and is important in acquiring a vocabulary.

■ The **visual-spatial scratchpad** holds and refreshes visual and/or spatial information and is used when, say, copying a drawing.

A recent addition, the **episodic buffer**, is the interface between the central executive, the two slave systems, and long-term memory. It is a storage system that helps bind elements together.

So why does size matter? An extensive research program in the U.S. has revealed strong correlations between working-memory capacity and tasks such as reading comprehension, and measures of general intelligence (see Topic 8.4). Test results show that individuals with high working-memory capacity regularly perform better than those with a low working-memory capacity.

Patients with a dense amnesia for everyday events have an unimpaired working memory and intellectual capacity.

A key contributor to working-memory capacity is the ability to focus and exclude distractions. Low working-memory capacity leads to less attentional control, which leads to greater distractibility, which in turn leads to low exam scores.

5.8 Language skills

Language is produced and understood using an infinitely long dictionary, with a fixed and finite set of rules for using the words at our disposal.

It is amazing to think we are, in principle, capable of understanding and producing an infinite number of novel utterances that can reflect an infinite number of thoughts.

A key concept of these language skills is the mental lexicon, a dictionary that stores information about the sounds of words, their pronunciations, and their meanings. We call upon this lexicon when listening to everyday speech. By extracting the sound of a word from speech and matching it with an entry in the lexicon, we are able to gain access to the word's meaning.

A grammar is a system of rules that specifies word order. It is internalized and used by the speaker to extract the meaning of a sentence in a process called **parsing**. This meaning is then combined with that of other sentences, and knowledge of the world, to produce a plausible interpretation of what is being said.

Auctioneers can speak at rates of more than five words per second and remain comprehensible.

When speaking, sentences are constructed in four stages: a conceptual stage; a word stage; a sound stage; and an articulatory stage. Two interacting processes are involved at each stage, one that produces a grammatically appropriate framework and one that fills the framework with the appropriate words. This is the basis of all language.

Stages of speech production

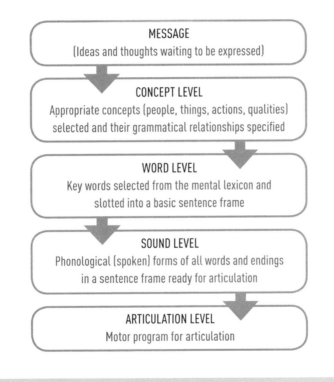

The above diagram outlines key stages in the
production of a spoken sentence (after Sterling,
2016, with some simplification).

5.9 Judgment and choice

We make judgments and choices more often by rules of thumb than by statistical or logical reasoning.

Suppose you were asked to judge the occupation of a person randomly selected from equal numbers of accountants, academics, and designers attending a conference. Opt for any one of them, say designer, and you base your decision on having a one-third chance of being right. However, if, on being told that the person is wearing a smart gray suit, you opt for accountant, your judgment is based on a rule of thumb: It is a **representative heuristic**, or stereotype, rather than based on the statistical information you possess.

Similarly, if asked to estimate the probability of a plane crash, your answer will be influenced by how recently a crash was on the news. This is because the event affects your availability to memory of scenes of carnage. You will have used the **availability heuristic**.

Choices or decisions are also made using rules of thumb. Nobel laureates Daniel Kahneman and Amos Tversky focused on biases in decision-making (1979; 1984). They showed that humans are risk averse when calculating prospective gains and risk seeking when calculating losses, and that framing the same choices in different ways can produce different decisions.

The diagnosis you receive from your doctor will be influenced by those of patients she or he has seen recently.

Current theory asserts that, depending on factors such as training, we use heuristics to make quick judgments and choices and reasoning to make more considered responses.

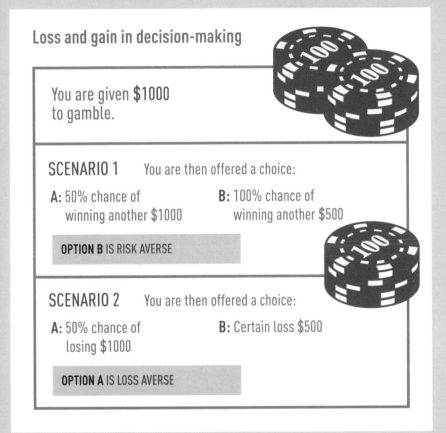

Loss and gain in decision-making

You are given **$1000**
to gamble.

SCENARIO 1   You are then offered a choice:

A: 50% chance of
winning another $1000

B: 100% chance of
winning another $500

OPTION B IS RISK AVERSE

SCENARIO 2   You are then offered a choice:

A: 50% chance of
losing $1000

B: Certain loss $500

OPTION A IS LOSS AVERSE

Nobel Laureates Daniel Kahneman and Amos Tversky showed that, in
decision-making involving uncertain outcomes, people avoid risk when
there are gains to be made and avoid loss when they could lose.

5.10 Reasoning

When we do not have
access to the bare
facts, we tend to turn
to reason. We do not
always do so within the
rules of logic, however.

We apply reasoning when we make inferences or draw
conclusions that go beyond the information available. For
example, if told that my taxes are going to increase I would
conclude that, if nothing else changes, my standard of living
is going to decline.

■ **Inductive reasoning** involves making an inference based
on existing knowledge. If told that birds have wings and that
slods are birds, we infer that slods have wings. However,
research has found that people's inductive inferences are
influenced by irrelevant characteristics such as typicality.
So, if told that birds have wings, we are quicker to agree that
robins have wings than penguins do, because robins are
more typical of the type of "bird."

■ **Deductive reasoning** is the process by which, given one
or more true premises, the reasoner draws a conclusion that
is necessarily true: All men have webbed feet and President
Obama is a man, therefore President Obama has webbed feet.
However, people don't always follow the rules of logic. Some
experiments have found belief bias—the fact that believable
conclusions are almost always accepted as being valid,
regardless of their actual validity.

■ **Scientific reasoning** involves hypothesis testing, which
requires a scientist to search for both supporting and
falsifying evidence (see opposite)

**Formal logic was
discovered independently
in Greece, China and India
over 2,000 years ago.**

The Wason selection task

If there is a vowel on one side of the card, there is an even number on the other side of the card. Test this statement by turning over as few cards as possible.

If someone is drinking beer they must be 21 or over. On each card there is a beverage and a corresponding age. Test the validity of this statement by turning over as few cards as possible.

Two versions of the same task are shown above. In both, the answer is the same two cards: The card farthest left verifies the rule; the card farthest right falsifies it. And yet people find the beer/coke version easier, because it uses a real-world situation rather than something more abstract.

LEARNING & EXPERTISE

XYZ

Although we have the capacity to solve the problems that confront us, learning provides us with the factual, procedural, and strategic knowledge we need to deal effectively with problems that recur. In some instances, we specialize in a particular type of problem and go on to become experts.

All learning begins as a problem that has to be solved, and our first topic outlines several commonly used strategies. Thereafter the chapter explores several types of learning.

Instrumental learning occurs when we learn—through trial and error—that some responses to a problematic situation are effective, while others are not. Observational learning demonstrates how we can save ourselves the time and effort required to learn from our mistakes, although hands-on experience is also needed for effective performance. At other times the complexity of a situation

Continues overleaf

needs a more cognitive approach, which might involve hypothesis testing or actively seeking new knowledge.

Learning can sometimes occur without an awareness of what we have learnt. This is called implicit learning. For example, we can all tie our laces without having to remember specifically how it is done each time. Classical conditioning is a type of simple implicit learning that is found across many species, while language learning is another type. It is complex and seems to be confined to the human species.

Although there are very different kinds of skills, all skill learning entails the same three stages of development. This begins with a conscious appraisal of what the skill entails and ends with a set of routines that execute it automatically. Finally, what use would any skills be to us without practice? We examine the key aspects of this and discover how some motivated learners go on to develop expertise in their chosen skill.

Contents

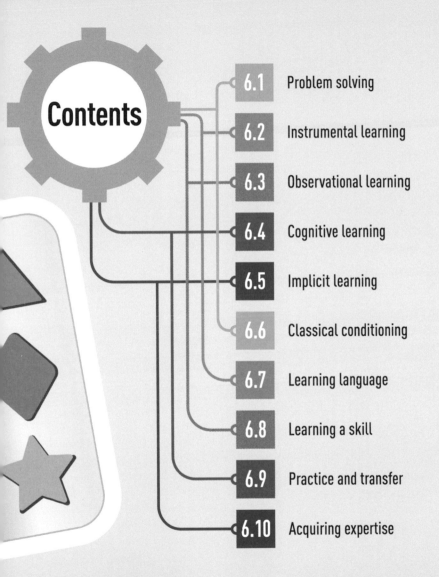

6.1 Problem solving

6.2 Instrumental learning

6.3 Observational learning

6.4 Cognitive learning

6.5 Implicit learning

6.6 Classical conditioning

6.7 Learning language

6.8 Learning a skill

6.9 Practice and transfer

6.10 Acquiring expertise

6.1 Problem solving

Problems are an inevitable part of our daily lives. Thankfully we have a number of effective strategies for solving them.

Problems can be classified as being well-defined, with a definite solution (sudoku), or ill-defined, with no clear solution (chess). Everyday problems are usually ill-defined. Here are some of the strategies we use:

- **Trial-and-error learning**: A series of, initially random, responses that become shaped by their outcomes. For example, figuring out how a new gizmo works. See Topic 6.2.

- **Problem solving by insight**: A sudden awareness of the solution—the "aha" moment. A restructuring of the problem follows.

- **Problem solving by analogy**: A current problem is solved by applying a previously successful solution to a similar problem. For example, managing a difficult person the way you managed someone similar a few months ago.

In 1959, Allen Newell and Herbert Simon produced the General Problem Solver computer program. The program conceptualized problem solving as a series of processes involved in moving from an initial problem state, through a problem space, to the goal state. This was achieved using strategies such as means-end analysis, in which the path to the goal is broken down into a set of more manageable subgoals. We often work in the same way, using one—or a combination of—the above strategies.

It took 40 years to develop a chess-playing computer (Deep Blue) able to defeat world champion Gary Kasparov in 1997.

The hobbits and orcs problem

Three hobbits and three orcs have to cross a river using a boat that can hold only two creatures. The number of orcs must never outnumber the number of hobbits. How many times do they cross the river and in what combination of hobbits and orcs?

Step	First bank	Who's in the boat		Second bank
START	HHHOOO			
1	HHOO	HO	⟹	HO
2	HHHOO	H	⟸	O
3	HHH	OO	⟹	OOO
4	HHHO	O	⟸	OO
5	HO	HH	⟹	HHOO
6	HHOO	HO	⟸	HO
7	OO	HH	⟹	HHHO
8	OOO	O	⟸	HHH
9	O	OO	⟹	HHHOO
10	HO	HO	⟸	HHOO
11		HO	⟹	HHHOOO

This solution to the above problem requires means-end analysis with insight at move six, because it seems to be taking a backward step.

6.2 Instrumental learning

Whether it's a gold star at school or a company bonus at Christmas time, we thrive on rewards for good behavior. Psychologists put this to good effect.

Building on the seminal work of Edward Thorndike, B. F. Skinner worked with pigeons to explore the parameters of instrumental learning (also known as trial-and-error learning; 1948).

He rewarded a pigeon with food for pecking a green key but not a red key. Eventually the pigeon learnt to peck only the green key. Skinner concluded that the reward reinforced the association between the appropriate stimulus (green) and the response, in this case, pecking.

Skinner and his followers then explored the idea further, to see if instrumental learning could change behavior. They demonstrated that rewards facilitated learning, but that punishment repressed behavior. Thus is has been found that the disorganized behavior of autistic children might, therefore, be shaped by rewarding positive behaviors, such as socializing, and ignoring negative ones, such as shouting.

Some claim that instrumental learning is always a nonconscious process (see Topic 6.5). However adult humans consciously use trial and error as a problem-solving strategy (see Topic 6.1). It is also in evidence in token economies—regimes that reward good behavior—when participants choose to comply or not. Token economies have been applied in education, mental health and prisons, with varying degrees of success.

Biofeedback can be used to reduce high blood pressure by signaling (rewarding) decreases in pressure.

Seven elements of a token economy

When working with autistic children, the following program has to be implemented by all the children's carers all of the time. It is intensely demanding.

TARGET BEHAVIORS	Select the desirable target behaviors to be strengthened.
TYPES OF TOKENS	Choose the tokens to be used as conditioned reinforcers (e.g. star stickers).
BACKUP REINFORCERS	Showcase the backup reinforcers to be exchanged for tokens (e.g. candy, free time).
REINFORCEMENT SCHEDULE	Set up a reinforcement schedule for token delivery (e.g. for every correct response).
EXCHANGE CRITERION	Decide how many tokens are needed to be exchanged for the backup reinforcers?
TIME/PLACE FOR EXCHANGE	Set a time and a place for exchanging tokens for backup reinforcers.
RESPONSE COST	Employ a penalty where tokens are taken away for engaging in inappropriate behaviors.

Here are the basic guidelines for setting up a token economy, as outlined by Miltenberger (2008). They were written with autistic children in mind.

6.3 Observational learning

We all have role models—people whose behavior or skills we'd like to emulate. We watch them and we learn.

Learning by observing others is an important tool. It allows an observer to adopt behaviors and learn skills that are productive, while ignoring those that are not. Observational learning can help to avoid dangers and minimizes failure.

A seminal paper by Albert Bandura showed that children imitated a model's aggression toward a large doll (1977). Subsequent work showed that imitation decreased if the model's behavior was punished. However, it seemed to make no difference whether the behavior was rewarded or not. Bandura argued that the likelihood of an observer repeating the behavior depended, firstly, on whether it was encoded in memory (see Topic 5.4) and secondly on whether there was sufficient motive.

Observational learning is found in a range of species. The probability of it happening is affected by characteristics such as the animal's social rank within its pack, gender, and age—of both the observer and the model. Animals are influenced by what the majority are doing, by successful individuals, and by kin.

Young macaques can develop a fear of snakes solely by observing parental fear.

Humans use observational learning to acquire motor skills and cognitive skills such as writing. In both cases the observer learns about the structure of the skill and how to coordinate its different components, including error detection. Then it is a question of perfecting the skill.

Conditions for observational learning

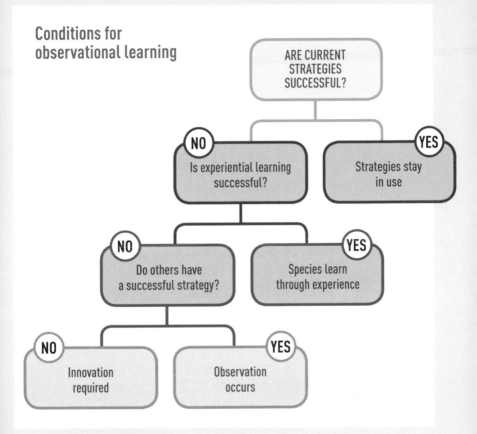

This decision tree describes when observational learning is most likely to occur (after Laland, 2004, with modifications). It does not depict decisions actually being made by an individual.

6.4 Cognitive learning

Remember how you were taught at school? Your teachers were helping you to learn through assimilation of material.

Cognitive learning involves the conscious use of strategies to acquire new knowledge. The focus here is on **hypothesis testing** and the **assimilation** of new material.

Humans often learn by formulating and testing hypotheses. For example, a pitcher may try several types of pitch to find a batter's weakness. Using observation and existing evidence, a hypothesis is formulated and tested against new evidence. The hypothesis is then accepted, rejected, or revised. People actively seek evidence that supports a hypothesis and will ignore or reject evidence that doesn't. This is widely evident in everyday life.

Assimilation of conceptually complex material is a cognitive learning strategy employed by students of all ages. Generally, if one does these things, there need not even be an intention to learn. It involves the following stages:

- Understanding the material.
- Organizing the material so that the different components are connected.
- Embedding the new material within existing knowledge.
- Testing one's knowledge of the material.

This, and hypothesis testing are just two methods of cognitive learning.

The systematic testing of scientific theories often starts with a laboratory accident. This was the case with both penicillin and classical conditioning.

Concept maps

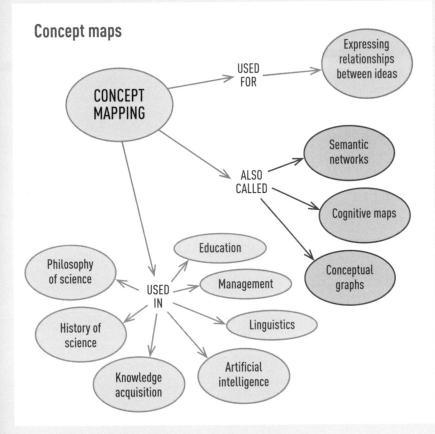

A concept map about concept maps! The principles of cognitive learning discussed opposite underpin the popular technique of learning by concept mapping.

6.5 Implicit learning

Every time you fasten a button on a shirt, skirt, or pair of pants, you do it without needing to recall how it is done.

Classical conditioning and instrumental learning in animals indicate that learning can occur without knowledge of what has been learnt. The evidence for **implicit learning** in humans is not so easy to obtain, because there is always the possibility that humans are aware of what they are learning.

- Tactics used to score by basketball players has been shown to be shaped by their history of success or failure. They are unaware of this, however.

- As both children and adults we learn and use hundreds of concepts expertly. However, we do this without an intention to learn and in many cases we are unable to define the concept learnt.

- An artificial grammar is a set of rules that generates sequences of letters, much like the grammar of a language generates sequences of words. Participants can learn to distinguish grammatical from ungrammatical sequences without being able to articulate the rules of the grammar.

- In a weather-forecasting experiment participants had to learn to predict rain from information such as cloud cover and recency of rainfall. Their predictions improved over time, yet they were unable to say how this happened (Knowlton et al 1996).

Although researchers have yet to identify the processes involved, all of the above examples suggest implicit learning.

People in conversation are often unaware that they have matched the amount of attention they allocate to others with the degree to which they agree with them.

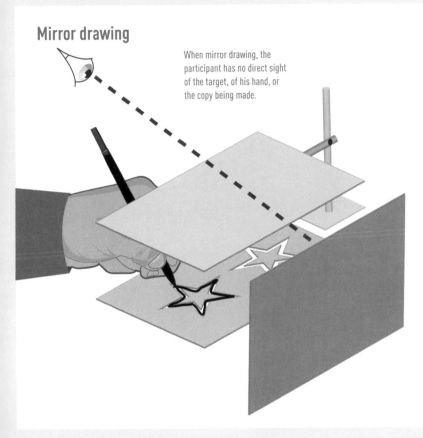

Mirror drawing

When mirror drawing, the participant has no direct sight of the target, of his hand, or the copy being made.

Mirror drawing is a procedural skill in which errors decrease with practice, showing learning. When the amnesic HM took part in the experiment he developed a skill over six months, but was completely unable to recall anything of the experiment—even after each day's trials.

6.6 Classical conditioning

Does your dog get excited when it hears the can opener being used?

A famous example of classical conditioning is that of Nobel Laureate Ivan Pavlov, who observed that dogs salivate naturally at the sight of food (1890s). He showed that salivation could be induced by a neutral stimulus—a bell sounding—if it was repeatedly paired with the sight of the food. Crucially, this occurred even in the absence of food.

Classical conditioning may be the basis of some phobias. Take the case of Little Albert, investigated by J. B. Watson (1920). The infant developed a fear response to furry objects, including some animals, after a loud startling noise had been paired with a previously neutral furry stimulus. However, many common phobias involve objects or situations that are fear-inducing for survival reasons anyway—say, snakes or heights—and their status as initially neutral stimuli is therefore questionable. These phobias may be just extreme versions of common responses.

Among other things, the principles of classical conditioning have been used to treat phobias. The idea here is to replace the stimulus-fear association with a stimulus-no-fear association using conditioning. Therefore, a person who is phobic to insects learns to replace the fear response—say, increased heart rate and sweating—with a calm response of normal heart rate and no sweating.

Patients who ate before chemotherapy, which induces nausea, developed an independent aversion to the foods eaten.

Pavlov's dogs

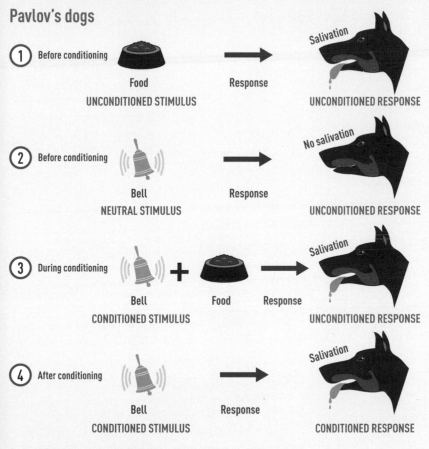

A simplified representation of the experiments Pavlov carried out with his dog. The illustrations demonstrate the different response elicited during the course of the trials.

6.7 Learning language

Children pick up language with remarkable ease and without any formal instruction. How do they do it?

The linguist Noam Chomsky is credited with one of the leading theories on learning language. Developed during the 1960s, his argument is based on the idea that humans are born with an innate ability to acquire a vocabulary and a system of rules (a grammar) for combining words.

In support of his theory of innateness, Chomsky cites the fact that, although we correct young children when using language, we do not explicitly teach them any rules of sentence structure.

Consistent with Chomsky's view, research over 50 years has found that nonhuman primates can be taught to use simple sentence structures. However, they only do so after years of intensive training. Furthermore, they attain, at best, the expertise of two- to three-year-old children. Despite this, psychologists maintain that the innateness explanation leaves too many questions unanswered.

Children become impressive communicators by age four without explicit coaching.

The search for an explanation has focused, instead, on a child's linguistic, conceptual, and social environment. Current thinking, therefore, is that caregiver language, or "motherese," contributes to acquisition by using simple vocabulary, short sentences, and exaggerated intonation and stress. It is this that helps children learn different word types and how sentences are structured.

The articulate chimp? This is a photograph of Nim Chimpsky, the subject of a language learning study. In contrast to the claims made about Washoe and other chimps, Nim's trainers disputed the claim that these primates could use even a simple grammar (Terrace et al. 1979).

6.8 Learning a skill

Whether you're into juggling, playing chess, or tap dancing, you'll learn a new skill in three distinct stages.

According to the Fitts-Anderson model of skills acquisition (1982) the three stages involved when learning a skill are the same, no matter what that skill is.

■ Stage 1: Known as the cognitive stage, this involves an appraisal of the task. What is the goal? What are the rules? What are its various components? This is followed by explicit attempts to put it all together. For example, learning the moves and rules of chess or learning how to hold the club and how to position your head and feet when putting.

■ Stage 2: The associative stage. The various components of the skill are smoothed into working combinations and sequences through practice (see Topics 6.9 and 6.10). So, putting the gear shift in drive, looking in the mirror, releasing the handbrake, depressing the gas pedal, and pulling away becomes a sequence that requires less and less thought.

■ Stage 3: The automatic stage, reached after extensive practice. Executing the skill is now on "autopilot." In many cases the performer can do something else at the same time without disruption—for example, driving and talking.

Skills learned may be as diverse as speaking Spanish or juggling, yet this process of appraisal– practice–autopilot–mode underpins all skills when it comes to learning,

As professional golfers know, thinking too much about an automated skill can severely disrupt its execution.

Skill types

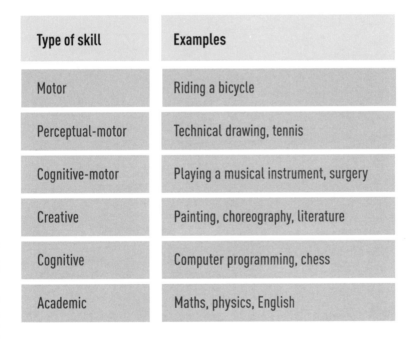

Type of skill	Examples
Motor	Riding a bicycle
Perceptual-motor	Technical drawing, tennis
Cognitive-motor	Playing a musical instrument, surgery
Creative	Painting, choreography, literature
Cognitive	Computer programming, chess
Academic	Maths, physics, English

Skill types can be listed as six major groups: motor, perceptual motor, cognitive motor, creative, cognitive, and academic.

6.9 Practice and transfer

The speed of learning, and its permanence, are affected by the amount and type of practice carried out.

Practice is indispensible for long-term learning. It reduces the number of errors made and the time taken to perform a given task. The effects of practice are seen in the ubiquitous learning curve shown opposite, which illustrates the three basic stages of learning a skill (see Topic 6.8).

Type of practice is important. **Distributed practice** involves several short sessions and produces more durable learning than **massed practice**, which is one long session. This holds for a variety of skills, from sports to learning a foreign vocabulary, and solving math problems. However, any student will tell you that cramming is very effective in the short term.

There is also **mixed practice** and **blocked practice**. A dancer learning a complex piece of choreography will remember it better in the long term if he or she practices the different components as a sequence (mixed practice). However, short-term performance may be better under blocked practice, where each component is practiced to automatized perfection separately.

Finally, it seems possible to transfer something learnt from one skill to another, saving both time and effort. There is some hard evidence from education studies where training in scientific thinking and research methods has been shown to improve students' ability to reason.

A man took nine years and many thousands of hours to recite *Paradise Lost* (10,565 lines) from memory.

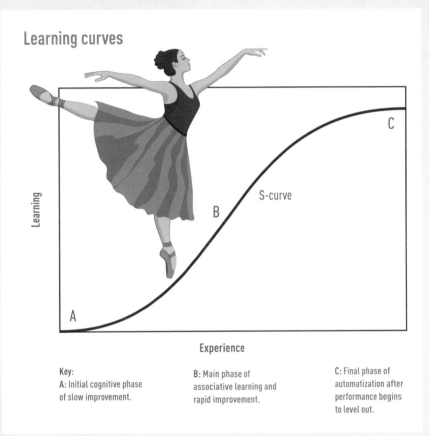

Learning curves

Learning

A

B

S-curve

C

Experience

Key:
A: Initial cognitive phase of slow improvement.

B: Main phase of associative learning and rapid improvement.

C: Final phase of automatization after performance begins to level out.

An idealized learning curve showing the three broad phases of skill acquisition. A child learning ballet from scratch will experience these three basic stages of learning. So, too, will a skilled ballerina getting to grips with new choreography.

6.10 Acquiring expertise

Is an expert physicist born with exceptional talent, or simply someone who works longer and harder at it?

Experts are generally thought of as being the product of ambition, hard work, and a specific aptitude of genetic origin (see Topic 8.5). It's a description that fits chess masters, athletes, and Nobel Prize winners.

However, since the 1990s, Anders Ericsson has taken the provocative view that experts are actually the product of an early start, dedication, and huge amounts of practice.

Studies of chess masters, physicists, and medics have shown that an expert's knowledge is organized in a way that enables instant recognition of, and response to, a range of situations. Experts tend to tackle problems head-on rather than working back from a solution. However, expertise is generally **domain** specific. In many cases, experts are pretty average in other fields.

Expertise develops through practice. Studies of musicians and chess players have found that top professionals have thousands of hours of practice behind them. Furthermore, those at the very top began their careers as children, with great support from their parents and good coaching.

Although he was a high achiever in physics and maths, there was little in Einstein's education to suggest world-changing genius.

Ericsson draws attention to the fact that experts are so designated by their peers. He argues for classification on the basis of objectively measured performance instead. Whatever the criteria, we may need to distinguish between expertise (concert musicians) and genius (Mozart).

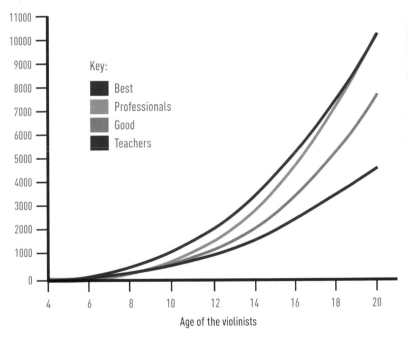

Practice makes perfect

Accumulated hours
of practice

Key:

- Best
- Professionals
- Good
- Teachers

Age of the violinists

Estimated amounts of practice by violinists who reach different levels
of expertise. (Krampe & Tesch-Römer, 1993)

MOTIVATION, STRESS, & EMOTION

This chapter is split into three broad sections of human behavior: motivation, stress, and emotion.

It begins with an overview of various psychologists' attempts to understand our basic needs and motivators.How do we choose which goals to pursue in life?

We then look at stress—a mental phenomena with which most of us are more than familiar. We explore firstly the physical effects of stress—the interaction between mind and body that occurs when we experience both positive and negative forms of stress. Then we examine the ways in which we appraise potentially stressful situations, and the stages we go through in order to cope with them.

This brings us to the idea of ego-depletion—the concept that we have a limited amount of self-control, which governs our ability to self-regulate and, when exhausted, needs to recharge.

Continues overleaf

These various motivators and drivers do not occur in a purely rational sense—we are emotive as well as cognitive beings, after all. As such we review the physiological and psychological effects of a few of the many emotions that characterize the human condition. Some of these are emotions we think of as negative—anger and the related emotions guilt, shame, and embarrassment. We also look at two more positive emotions: joy and love.

Finally, we round this chapter off with an exploration of situations when cold logical cognition meets hot emotional cognition. How do these processes interact with one another and how do they play out in research on moral decision-making?

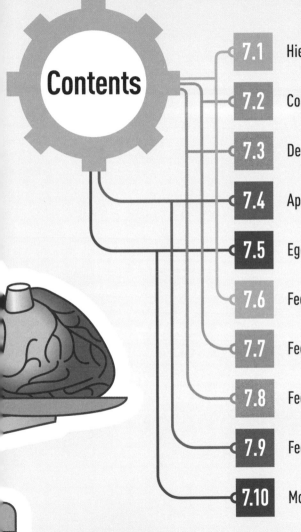

Contents

7.1 Hierarchy of needs

7.2 Complex motivation

7.3 Defining stress

7.4 Appraising stress

7.5 Ego depletion

7.6 Feelings of anger

7.7 Feelings of guilt

7.8 Feelings of joy and happiness

7.9 Feelings of love

7.10 Moral dilemmas

7.1 Hierarchy of needs

What's driving you as you journey toward your full potential as a human being?

We have a hierarchy of needs, from straightforward physical demands for food and warmth to more complex needs like fulfilling our wishes and desires.

Abraham Maslow (1943) suggests that basic needs must be met before we can aim to fulfill higher ones. Basic needs comprise physiological and safety needs, love, and belonging:

- **Physiological needs** are the things we need simply to survive—air, water, clothes.

- **Safety needs** relate to personal and financial security and good health.

- **The need for love and belonging** is fulfilled via membership to social groups or relationships with others.

Once these needs are satisfied, higher level needs come into play. These reflect a need to feel positive about ourselves and for others to feel positive about us, too. In the original formulation of Maslow's model, the highest motivator of all is **self-actualization**—the fulfillment of all of one's potential as a human being.

Work by Goebel and Brown suggests young adults seem to have the highest need for self-actualization (1981).

Research has established that each of these needs exists, yet Maslow's theories are hard to test empirically. However, his theories have done much to inform the development of attachment theory and positive psychology.

Toward self-actualization

High needs

Self-actualization

Esteem

Love and belonging

Safety and security

Physiological

Low needs

Abraham Maslow's hierarchy of needs (1943) differentiates between higher and basic needs. Our motivation to behave can be driven by multiple needs at the same time.

7.2 Complex motivation

What motivates us frequently comes down to a balancing act between costs and likely rewards.

Some of our actions are directly motivated by our direct needs (see Topic 7.1), but what motivates us beyond that? Victor Vroom put forward a theory known as the Valance, Instrumentality, and Expectancy approach (VIE, 1964; see opposite) to help explain complex motivation.

The VIE approach argues that the strength of any given motivation—say, to exercise or to attend a party—is defined by the way the following factors interact:

- **Valence**: How attractive is the action to a person? What reward will it bring?

- **Instrumentality**: The idea that the action, if performed successfully, will lead to receiving the reward.

- **Expectancy**: The belief that exerting the effort required will lead to a successful performance.

This approach helps explain why we choose to act in different ways, depending on a given situation. Essentially, it involves a weighing up of the likely outcome of our actions by how much we want it, how easy it is to act, and how likely we are to achieve our ends. On one occasion, therefore, a person may be motivated by a high probability of success for a low-value reward. This is the easy option. On another occasion, a lower probability of a high-value reward might appeal—the hard-but-rewarding option.

If achievable, setting a challenging, specific target should be more motivating than a vague one.

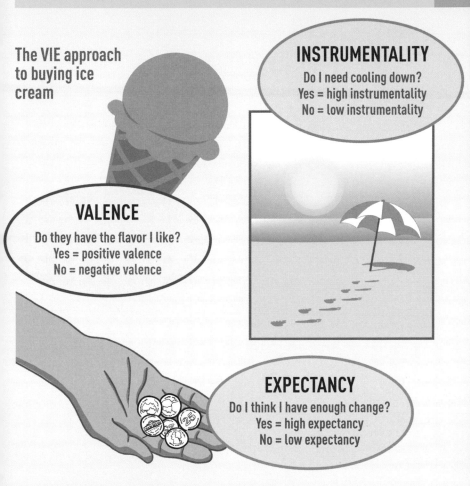

The VIE approach to buying ice cream

INSTRUMENTALITY
Do I need cooling down?
Yes = high instrumentality
No = low instrumentality

VALENCE
Do they have the flavor I like?
Yes = positive valence
No = negative valence

EXPECTANCY
Do I think I have enough change?
Yes = high expectancy
No = low expectancy

Sometimes we choose to perform a given behavior based on the extent we expect that behavior to provide a valued outcome. At other times the choice is based on the likelihood we can achieve the behavior.

7.3 Defining stress

Rapid heart beat, flushed face, dry mouth, sweaty palms. Who isn't familiar with these symptoms of a stressful situation?

Stress is a form of psychological and/or physiological arousal that drives behavior. It can affect us in two ways:

- **Eustress** provides a challenge and enables us to perform better.

- **Distress** generally has a negative outcome, inhibiting performance and causing negative emotions such as anxiety. It can also lead to negative physical outcomes that include heart disease.

Stressors include the experience or threat of: crises and catastrophes; major life events (marriage, bereavement); and a host of day-to-day hassles. Physiologically it has a number of common effects, the majority of which are governed by the hypothalamus.

When a stress response is triggered, this area of the brain activates the production of adrenaline—ready for a fight or flight response. Among other effects, this increases heart rate, causes sweating and other functions that may be useful in responding to an immediate threat. It also activates the production of cortisol, which helps maintain blood sugar supply, reduces swelling in response to injury, but also suppresses immune responses.

While we respond to stress in the same ways physiologically, our psychological responses are down to the individual, as you'll see in the following topic.

> **For many people, one response to long-term stress is a reduction in digestion, leading to a smaller appetite.**

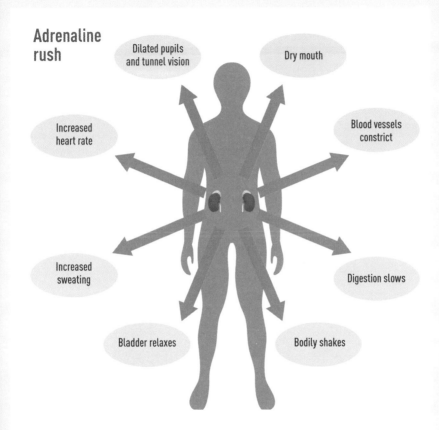

Adrenaline rush

Dilated pupils and tunnel vision

Dry mouth

Increased heart rate

Blood vessels constrict

Increased sweating

Digestion slows

Bladder relaxes

Bodily shakes

Adrenaline is produced by the adrenal glands, which sit just above the kidneys. It affects many parts of the body, making us faster, more alert, and generally more able to engage in fight or flight responses.

7.4 Appraising stress

You are petrified of dogs and come face to face with a snarling, teeth-baring canine. What do you do next?

Why is a situation stressful to one person, but not to another? Lazarus and Folkman's transactional theory of stress and coping (1984) attempts to answer this. At its core is the idea that we adopt certain strategies when appraising stress. Primarily we ask ourselves, what does this situation mean to me? Is it:

- A challenge: Something I can benefit from?
- A harm or loss: Something that has caused me distress?
- A threat: Something that could harm me in the future?

If we appraise the situation as threatening, we then make a secondary appraisal as to whether or not we can cope with it with the resources at our disposal. If we feel we can, we experience positive stress; if not, we experience negative stress (see Topic 7.3).

Coping strategies are also influenced by these appraisals. If we feel we have control over a problem, we are more likely to engage in problem-based strategies to change the situation—we actively seek solutions. When we feel the situation is beyond our control, we may engage in emotion-based strategies to reduce our negative emotional state.

Lazarus and Folkman's journal paper on this subject has been cited over 36,000 times!

Either way, both kinds of strategies are effective when it comes to minimizing the impact of the problem in the short term, at least.

A stressful encounter?

A SITUATION IS ENCOUNTERED
A boy cycling home hears a dog barking wildly in the distance.

SCENARIO 1
The dog is not visible. The boy has a fear of dogs and not being able to see it makes the situation worse. On his primary appraisal, the boy perceives a threat.

As the dog comes into view, the boy realizes it belongs to one of his neighbors. It must be lost. The sight of the boy calms the dog. The boy makes a secondary appraisal and feels able to cope.

SCENARIO 2
Even though the boy cannot see the dog, the barking sounds familiar. He thinks it might be the dog of his neighbor, who is usually playful. The boy perceives no threat. No secondary appraisal is necessary.

Lazarus and Folkman's model suggests we make a primary appraisal about the threat a situation presents and a secondary appraisal on our ability to cope. These define if, and how, we experience stress.

7.5 Ego depletion

Resist that chocolate bar before shopping for clothes and you may lack the willpower to resist the salesperson trying to sell you a pricier pair of jeans.

Roy Baumeister's work on ego depletion suggests that if you exert self-control in one context—say, by giving a speech in favor of a subject on which you disagree—you are likely to reduce self-control in subsequent, unrelated tasks, such as resisting eating a chocolate bar. Or if you succumb to several small temptations, you may not have the willpower to resist a larger, or more important one.

Willpower is thought to be similar to a muscle that can tire, but that can also be trained. It seems likely that we hold reserves of willpower for high-priority situations. Some theoreticians argue that this self-control is linked to levels of glucose in the body and suggest that consuming glucose-rich products, therefore, can replenish willpower.

Alternative models suggest that ego depletion reflects a shift in motivation from a desire for control to one of gratification. Either way, the condition has been linked to a variety of effects. They include:

- Reduced experience of guilt, which requires self-control
- Increased calorie intake among dieters
- Lowered mental determination among athletes

Ego depletion effects may be age-constrained. While most research has been conducted on undergraduates, some studies have failed to show the effects of ego depletion among people over 40.

Ego depletion can make a consumer more persistent and willing to pay more for a desirable product.

Resisting temptation . . . or not

Avoiding expending willpower in small decisions can lead to greater willpower being available for more important ones. "Sweating the small stuff" reduces the ability to exert control when we need it most.

7.6 Feelings of anger

Anger is an emotion we all recognize, but it is complex to define.

Increased heart rate and blood pressure, adrenal responses, and short breaths—these are all marks of an angry person. They are similar physiological markers to those of other emotions, such as fear, however, anger has different behavioral outcomes.

Facial expressions linked to anger appear innate and culturally universal: a tightening of the lips, bared teeth, eyebrows pulled down toward the bridge of the nose. Body posture can become wider with raised arms and a front-facing stance. Cognitive effects might include increased bias against others, greater optimism, and less awareness of risk.

Behavior ranges from passive aggression (ignoring someone) to uncontrolled violence. Scientists have attempted to map the characteristics of such responses. For example, Ephrem Fernandez argues that anger can vary across six dimensions: the direction, causes, reaction, characteristics, impulsivity, and objectivity (2008).

When angry, people seem to rely more on stereotypes when evaluating others.

While other, simpler, taxonomies exist, it is clear that anger is a highly complex state. People may seek anger management training, usually **cognitive behavioral therapy** (CBT) to help deal with it. This assumes that angry responses are based on erroneous appraisals of situations (see Topic 7.4) and that rectifying how you think can improve behavioral control.

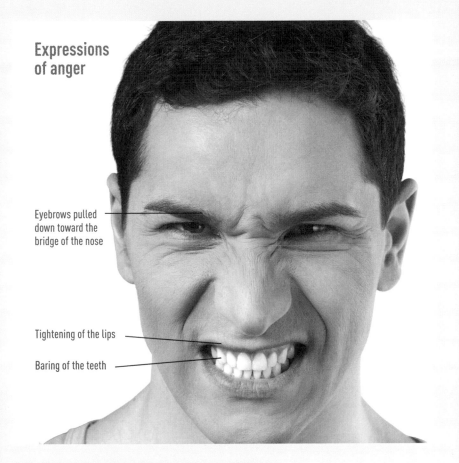

Expressions of anger

Eyebrows pulled down toward the bridge of the nose

Tightening of the lips

Baring of the teeth

While it is hard to map and define anger precisely, CBT-type approaches can help people control, not only their response to situations that get them angry, but also their resultant behavior.

7.7 Feelings of guilt

When we show that we are feeling guilty or embarrassed, those we have offended are almost automatically disposed to react more favorably.

We are social creatures who rely on being part of a group to thrive. The emotion of guilt appears to serve the function of regulating our behavior.

Shame and embarrassment have a role to play here, too. The former enables us to show contrition for acts that violate social norms, while the latter allows us to demonstrate that such acts may not be intentional. Such emotions do not appear to be present at birth, but seem culturally universal.

Embarrassment has a number of facial expressions that are recognized cross-culturally. These include blushing, avoiding eye contact, and looking down or to the left. These facial displays can be effective in ameliorating negative responses in others—for example, people punish others less if they show embarrassment. Feelings of guilt also seem to increase subsequent levels of cooperation in experimental settings—even among those who usually avoid such behavior—while levels of anticipated shame predict adherence to organizational rules.

Many animals gesture embarrassment using their faces and bodies, but blushing appears only among humans.

Although these emotions appear universal, the extent to which they appear varies across cultures. Emiko Kobayash and colleagues have demonstrated that Japanese workers in their studies anticipated more shame from breaking the rules than did American workers (2001).

Seeking forgiveness

Reik and colleagues (2014) suggest that guilt is predicted by the extent we feel committed to the victim, take responsibility for, and think about, the transgression. The greater the guilt, the more we seek forgiveness.

7.8 Feelings of joy and happiness

It is hard to pinpoint, but a certain sense of well-being comes with feeling joyful.

The physiological markers of joy are not well understood. The emotion can lead to both heightened and calmed physiological states, but is often linked to increased endorphin production. Happiness is a similar emotion, but is seen as less intense and a longer term phenomenon—more of a mood than an emotion.

Joy does not always lead to smiles and laughter, but they are not uncommon. True smiles are called Duchenne smiles and involve an upturned mouth, raised cheeks, and a crinkling of the face around the corners of the eyes. They are often brief in duration. Newborn babies don't engage in Duchenne smiles, but start to at around six to eight weeks in response to social stimuli.

The scientific study of positive emotions such as joy and happiness is not as advanced as that of negative emotions. This is changing thanks to the scientific movement known as Positive Psychology. This gained real traction in 1998 when leading psychologist Martin Seligman highlighted the discipline's focus on mental illness at the expense of attempting to improve the lives of everyday people.

Nearly 20 years on, this movement has led to the study of various positive emotions and states, such as the feeling of "flow" you experience when everything appears to happen effortlessly.

Simulating the activation of the muscles involved in Duchenne smiles can improve mood!

The Duchenne smile

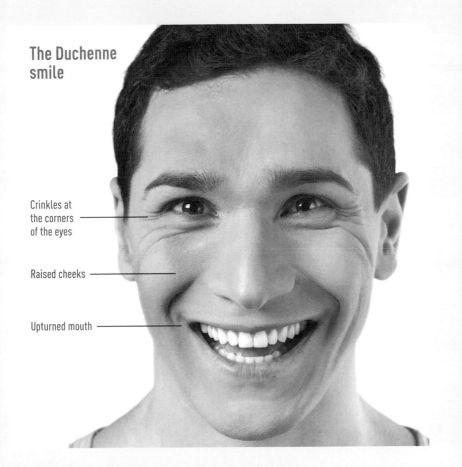

Crinkles at the corners of the eyes

Raised cheeks

Upturned mouth

We spend much of our time smiling, but the Duchenne smile is the only truly genuine form. It is also one of the earliest forms of social communication available to babies.

7.9 Feelings of love

Are you a passionate lover or a companionate one? Perhaps you are both. Your feelings depend on the type of relationship you are in.

Researchers have discovered that being in love seems to generate other biological responses. For example experiencing the feeling of love generates activity in associated neurotransmitters such as dopamine and oxytocin (see Topic 2.4). According to Elaine Hatfeld, love can be divided into two main groups (1987):

■ Passionate love involves deep, intense emotions, and, often, symptoms such as increased cardiac activity and other physical arousal.

■ Companionate love involves feelings that are deep, but less exciting, physically.

In general, it is thought that companionate love can emerge from passionate love and, typically, is more stable. How long love lasts varies across cultures. In 2012, reported divorce rates in Belgium were 2.81 per 1,000 people, in contrast to Singapore (1.3). Arranged marriages and love marriages vary, too. Social scientists Usha Gupta and Pushpa Singh report that, initially, love rates higher in love marriages than in arranged ones. But these ratings decrease in love marriages after two to five years and remain largely stable in arranged marriages for more than a decade (2009).

Research suggests that seeing pictures of romantic love activates reward pathways in the brain.

There is no question that love can be lasting, but it varies within relationships, depending on the circumstances.

Six types of love

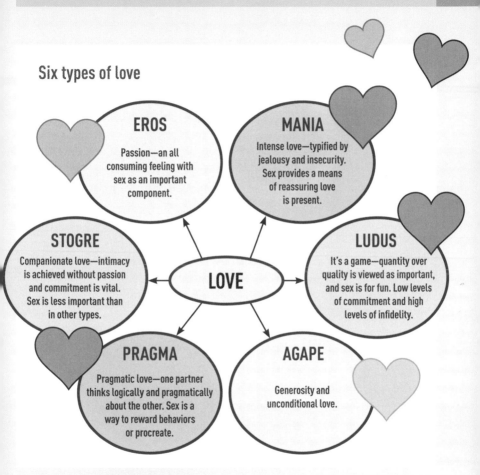

EROS

Passion—an all consuming feeling with sex as an important component.

MANIA

Intense love—typified by jealousy and insecurity. Sex provides a means of reassuring love is present.

STOGRE

Companionate love—intimacy is achieved without passion and commitment is vital. Sex is less important than in other types.

LOVE

LUDUS

It's a game—quantity over quality is viewed as important, and sex is for fun. Low levels of commitment and high levels of infidelity.

PRAGMA

Pragmatic love—one partner thinks logically and pragmatically about the other. Sex is a way to reward behaviors or procreate.

AGAPE

Generosity and unconditional love.

In the 1980s, scientists such as John Alan Lee, Clyde Hendrick, and Susan Hendrick argued that there are many types of love, all of which have different emotional and cognitive features.

7.10 Moral dilemmas

When and how do we use emotions to address moral dilemmas?

Scientists explore the way we behave using problems such as the footbridge and track dilemmas, first introduced by Philippa Foot in 1967.

Imagine you are on a footbridge and see a train about to run into a crowd. Standing next to you is a large man. Pushing him onto the tracks will stop the train, saving the others, but killing the large man. Would you push him? Few participants say they would. Now imagine you can move the points of the rail so the train avoids hitting the people on one track, but hits a single person on another. Many people say they would switch the points.

Why the difference? Research suggests that actively pushing someone off a bridge involves emotional responses while choosing a crowd of people over one (when both are possible) is a more rational, cognitive response. In support of this, thinking about the footbridge dilemma seems to activate emotional areas of the brain, while the track dilemma activates areas largely associated with abstract reasoning.

Other thought experiments include portraying the large man as evil, as a loved one, or as a child.

Additional studies have demonstrated that arousing participants' emotions by showing them a virtual-reality simulation of the single victim realizing his or her fate, reduces the frequency in which he or she is sacrificed.

What would you do?

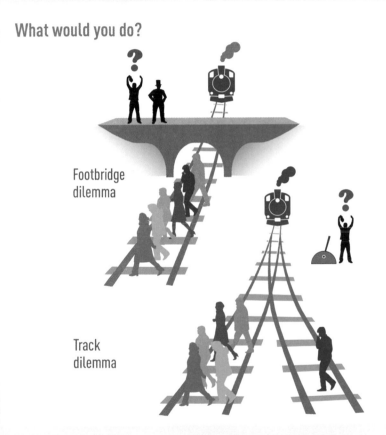

Footbridge
dilemma

Track
dilemma

The footbridge and track dilemmas appear superficially similar, but
seem to evoke different cognitive, neurological effects. These, in turn,
generate differing behavioral intentions.

GROUPS & INDIVIDUALS

N otwithstanding differences in age, gender, and culture, we share many character traits with other people. We do much the same things in much the same ways and for much the same reasons. However, although we are all members of a herd, each of us is also a unique combination of characteristics that merit study in their own right.

These characteristics are the focus of this chapter. We start by looking at the various methods used to study our uniqueness, including the Q-sort. Some of these have been developed into psychological tests in which our performance is measured against others to see how we compare to the population as a whole. These tests can measure things as diverse as likes and dislikes, hopes and fears, skills and intelligence.

Although differences in personality are readily observed, can we really be sure that they are biologically inherited or do

Continues overleaf

they arise as and when they are needed, depending on the situation? One thing that seems sure is that general intelligence is measurable and can be a reflection of a person's intellectual potential. A notion that complements general intelligence is aptitude—which skills can we say we are really good at? And which not?

The final sections of this chapter consider three diverse topics and their influence on our social behavior. The first is culture. Why is so much psychological research based on Western populations, for example, and how can we redress the balance? The second topic examines the notion that genes determine gender-related behavior and sexuality. And the third looks at what we consider normal behavior. When do people veer away from this norm to become exceptional or, in extreme cases, psychologically pathological?

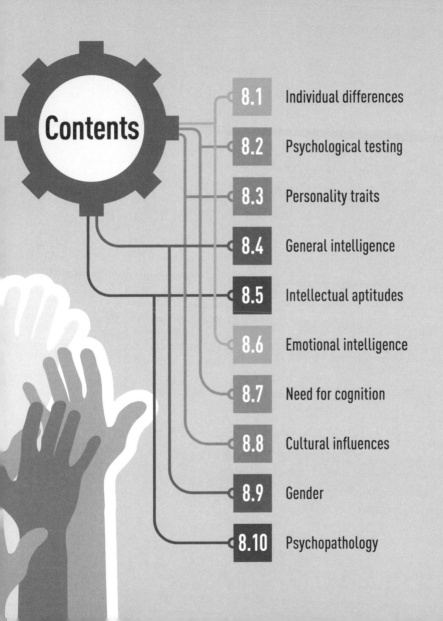

Contents

8.1 Individual differences

8.2 Psychological testing

8.3 Personality traits

8.4 General intelligence

8.5 Intellectual aptitudes

8.6 Emotional intelligence

8.7 Need for cognition

8.8 Cultural influences

8.9 Gender

8.10 Psychopathology

8.1 Individual differences

Most psychology is herd psychology, but surely there are some things that make us stand out from the crowd?

Various methods exist for studying individuals. These identify and document characteristics to see how a person differs from his/her peers. They include the following:

- The **dimensional approach**. Using standardized tests of ability and personality, an individual is compared to his/her peers on a number of dimensions. These include whether he or she is clever, poorly motivated, extrovert, and so on. This approach is used extensively in the selection of personnel (see Topic 10.4) and more selectively in education.

- The **self-referential approach**: In the Q-sort, a participant must sort 100 self-referent descriptions into nine categories from least to most typical of themselves (see opposite). Descriptions might include "I am shy," or "I am ambitious." This approach is used in clinical psychology and psychiatry.

- **Single-case methodology**. This uses a combination of interviews, observations, and standardized and bespoke tests to profile an individual. When compared to a control group of peers, important differences become evident. This approach is used extensively in psychiatry and clinical neuropsychology.

These methods are **idiographic**—they are concerned with individuals and their uniqueness. This is relatively rare in psychology, which is largely **nomothetic** and usually looks for herd-like generalizations.

Einstein's brain was removed, dissected, and distributed to researchers without permission. With his estate's approval, sections are displayed in the Mutter Museum, Philadelphia.

Example of a Q-sort

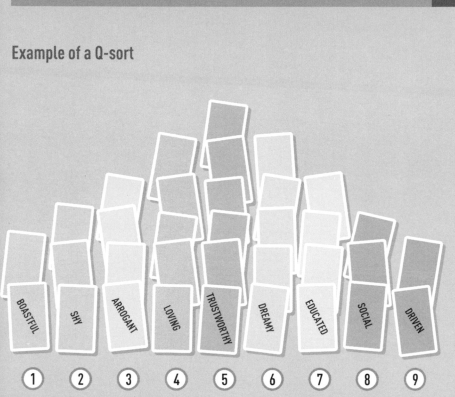

In the Q-sort, an individual places traits on a scale from 1 to 9. This person, for example, rates himself as very social and driven, and not particularly boastful or shy.

The Q-sort is used for a wide variety of research. It is useful when assessing individuals, since it provides an entirely subjective viewpoint of one's own traits.

8.2 Psychological testing

Rigorous analysis of your personality traits and abilities allows psychologists to assess your place in the normal distribution.

Psychological testing assumes that it is possible to characterize an individual in terms of personality traits, abilities, attitudes, skills, and behaviors. Such characteristics are deemed measurable. A key assumption is that each one is normally distributed in the general population (see opposite).

Tests consist of questions or statements addressing every aspect of the characteristic in question. For example, a test of extroversion would include "Do you like going out?," "Do you like being alone?," and so on. These tests have to fulfill a number of criteria:

■ They have to be reliable, in that a result is consistent when given to the same person on different occasions.

■ They have to be valid: They must measure what they purport to measure and be used to make accurate predictions about the testee.

■ They have to resist biases. For example, ability tests, say in math, may reflect intensive schooling, while attitude tests are susceptible to socially desirable responding. Allowances have to be made and estimates of the biases built in.

Psychological tests are used extensively in personnel selection to fit the person to the job; in education to assess a child's abilities; and in clinical psychology to assess an individual's problems and deliver appropriate treatment.

Written exams were used in China 2,000 years ago to determine fitness for office in civil law, the military, agriculture, and revenue.

The normal distribution

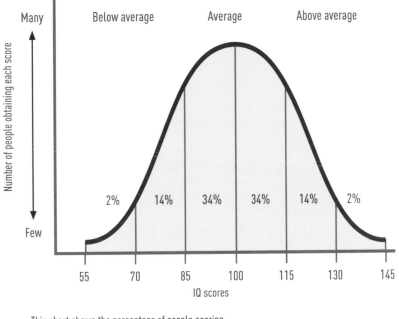

This chart shows the percentage of people scoring
in each segment under the normal curve.

If we give any test to a very large random sample and plot the frequency
with which each score occurs, we obtain a bell-shaped curve. Most
people locate in the middle with ever fewer toward the extremities.

8.3 Personality traits

What's your personality like? Take a look at the 16 personality traits opposite. How many of them describe you?

We talk about personality all the time. It is useful for describing people and for getting along socially. However, it has proved remarkably difficult to describe and measure personality objectively.

Raymond Cattell's work in the 1940s illustrates the concept of personality as a hierarchical structure. He used common words (lively, anxious, careful) and a statistical technique called factor analysis to identify 16 personality traits. He narrowed these down to five broader traits, which became precursors of the universally accepted **Big Five**. More recent work has used the same technique to identify a single General Factor of Personality, which is concerned with socially desirable behavior (see opposite).

How can we define personality? One view is that they are biologically inherited: An extrovert is someone who needs to increase a generally low level of arousal by seeking out social stimulation. An alternative early view was that behavior is determined entirely by the situation and that the consistency of behavior we call personality is illusory.

Subsequent research has shown, however, that behavior is predicted by personality, by the situation, and by the interaction of the two. So, an honest person will be less tempted in a given situation than a dishonest person, but may still succumb.

Extroversion and agreeableness are the traits most likely to be seen in other animals.

Hierarchy of personality traits

THE GENERAL PERSONALITY FACTOR
Social desirability

THE BIG FIVE PERSONALITY FACTORS
Emotional stability • Extroversion • Openness
Agreeableness • Conscientiousness

CATTELL'S 16 PERSONALITY FACTORS
Warm • Abstract thinker • Emotionally stable • Dominant
Enthusiastic • Conscientious • Bold • Tender-minded
Suspicious • Imaginative • Shrewd • Apprehensive
Experimenting • Self-sufficient • Controlled • Tense

A hypothesized hierarchy of personality traits. Personality can be described at different levels of detail. Someone assessing a personality—say, during a job interview—will select the level that best suits his/her purpose.

8.4 General intelligence

How quickly can you find the correct card in the opposite example? Tasks like this feature frequently in IQ tests.

General intelligence (Charles Spearman, 1904) is the common factor determining performance in tasks of understanding, reasoning, problem solving, and learning.

It is measured using time-constrained tests with abstract materials that increase in difficulty. An example is the Raven's Progressive Matrices (see opposite). Performance is expressed as an "intelligence quotient" (IQ) that is compared with that of the individual's peer group. Intelligence, as indicated by IQ, is assumed to be distributed in the normal population as a bell-shaped curve (see page 185).

The question is how to interpret differences in IQ? For example, do observed differences between social groups signify real intellectual differences? This raises further questions. Is intelligence genetically determined, for example? Or do the results reflect cultural bias and education? Whatever the answers, there is no doubt that one's IQ is a powerful predictor of academic success and general achievement over one's lifetime.

A key criticism of IQ performance is that it says nothing about the mechanisms underlying differences. Whether intelligent performance on a given task owes more to working memory (see Topic 5.7), more focused attention, or speedier access to knowledge remains to be addressed.

IQ in the general population has increased significantly over the last century.

The Raven's Progressive Matrices

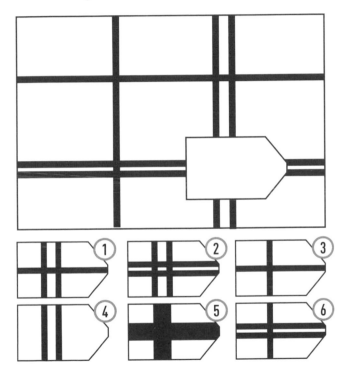

The task here requires the testee to pick the correct pattern from the
six alternatives to fit the blank space. The test is time-constrained and
gets progressively harder. The final score is a measure of IQ.

8.5 Intellectual aptitudes

We tend to favor subjects for which we have a natural ability. Aptitude may also influence our occupations in adult life.

General intelligence is just one approach to the study of individual differences (see also, Topics 8.1 and 8.4). A complementary idea is that people can be characterized in terms of a number of independent intellectual aptitudes.

An aptitude is a natural ability to acquire or learn a skill or competence. A person with an aptitude for math will find it easier than most to learn mathematical skills; a person with a musical aptitude will find it easier to learn a musical instrument, and so on. People have different aptitudes so the argument is that individuals can be characterized in terms of their aptitudinal profile.

A broader conception of aptitude comes from Howard Gardner's notion of multiple intelligences (1983). He initially identified seven intelligences, each with examples of target occupations served by that intelligence (see opposite). Gardner saw these intelligences as independent **biopsychological** potentials—an idea that is consistent with the observation that brain injury can damage some faculties but leave others intact (see Topic 2.6).

Although Gardner's theory has been influential in education, critics have argued that the intelligences (aptitudes) he identifies are either well established already or somewhat ad hoc.

Savants are people with a single outstanding ability (say, musical) against a background of profound intellectual impairment.

Multiple intelligences

INTELLIGENCE	END STATE/OCCUPATION
Logical-mathematical	Scientist, mathematician
Linguistic	Poet, journalist
Musical	Composer, violinist
Spatial	Navigator, sculptor
Bodily-kinesthetic	Dancer, athlete
Interpersonal	Therapist, salesman
Intrapersonal	Self-knowledge, yogi

Gardner's multiple intelligences (circa 1989) and the kind of profession
to which each is best suited.

8.6 Emotional intelligence

How good are you at reading other people's faces? Having a good grasp of our emotions is essential to building successful relationships.

Emotional intelligence refers to both a cognitive ability and a personality trait. As such, it is embodied in the following two independent concepts:

- **Ability emotional intelligence** is the cognitive ability to: perceive emotions correctly; to reason accurately when emotions are involved; to understand the relationships between emotions and how they change; and to manage emotions effectively. Such ability might be tested using the following test question: A manager gives an employee unexpected negative feedback in front of the team. How do you think the employee might feel? Providing an answer to this clearly requires cognitive ability.

- **Trait emotional intelligence** is a personality trait and is considered independent of intellectual ability, in the same way that other personality traits are. It involves perception of one's emotional self. A test of this trait might challenge adaptability, the ability to express emotion, social awareness, optimism, and others. The trait is argued to be independent from the Big Five personality traits but it does correlate with the General Factor of Personality (see Topic 8.3).

Emotional intelligence demonstrates that humans are social animals whose ability to relate to others is heavily dependent on the ability to understand the emotions that affect their relationships.

Special brain systems for processing identity, sexual attraction, and emotional state have evolved in nonhuman animals.

Perception of emotion

Coy

Confused

Anguished

Angry

Happy

Sad

Amused

Skeptical

Surprised

The ability to perceive emotions correctly is an indicator of emotional intelligence. Different cultures perceive basic emotions in the same way, suggesting that this aspect of emotional intelligence is universal.

8.7 Need for cognition

Do you seem to spend endless hours trying to make sense of the world around you?

Why do some people seem to need to think about things a lot, while others try to avoid effortful thinking? Psychologists suggest that this is due to an individual difference called need for cognition (NFC).

NFC individuals need to think in-depth about things in order to understand what is going on in their lives, and in the lives of others. They may display one, or several, of the following behaviors:

■ They may be more likely to be persuaded by relevant arguments (see Topic 4.4).

■ High NFC individuals tend to be more resistant to biases based on heuristics. Instead they are more affected by biases that appear rational (see Topic 4.5).

■ While people low in NFC seem to rely more on stereotypes, those with higher levels of NFC seem to relate more to personality traits—for example openness to experience and conscientiousness (see Topics 4.3 and 8.3).

■ NFC is linked to lowered levels of social anxiety and the ability to become "absorbed" in tasks.

People high in need for cognition are more likely to create false memories (see Topic 10.7)

Overall, need for cognition is an individual difference, which begins to explain why some enjoy pondering an idea and some do not. It also explains some of the cognitive effects (and biases) this trait is linked to.

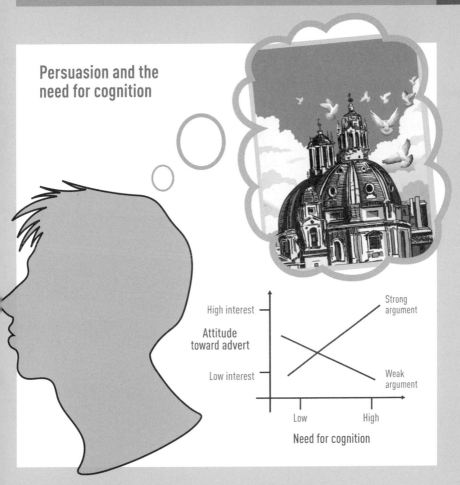

Persuasion and the need for cognition

High interest

Attitude
toward advert

Low interest

Strong
argument

Weak
argument

Low   High

Need for cognition

When faced with an advert, people higher in need for cognition will be
more affected by strong rather than weak arguments. People low in
need for cognition will be broadly equally affected by both types.

8.8 Cultural influences

Often overlooked in mainstream psychology, culture is, nevertheless, a powerful influence.

A major criticism of psychology, explored by Joe Heinrich, Steven Heine, and Ara Norenzayan, is that the majority of research is conducted on people who can be described as Western, educated, industrialized, rich, and democratic (W.E.I.R.D.). The effects of broader cultural influences are relatively understudied.

Hazel Markus and Alana Conner argue that culture influences us via the "Four I's," and that these influences cannot be ignored. They involve:

- How we perceive ourselves as Individuals.

- How people and social objects Interact (via mediums as diverse as media, public messages, architecture).

- The Institutions that develop and enforce social norms and laws (schools, churches, governments).

- The Ideas that underpin all of the points that influence us. Each of us influences these factors, too (allowing cultural evolution).

When compared to global populations, W.E.I.R.D. participants are often outliers on many measures.

When considering the individual, however, culture generates significant differences in cognition and behavior. Research on attributions, for example, typically shows that our perception of certain behaviors is biased by disposition (see Topic 4.5). However, outside W.E.I.R.D cultures, this effect is much reduced.

Individualism and collectivism

Cognition and behavior

Individualism

Independence
Individual effort and rewards
Responsibility for self

Collectivism

Interdependence
Team effort and rewards
Responsibility toward others

Culture

Collectivist and individualistic cultures have different views of the self, including levels of individual agency. These influence the ways in which people think and behave. Understanding these cultural effects is vital to a full understanding of psychological phenomena.

8.9 Gender

Is gender biologically determined or shaped by social influences?

The term biological gender consists of features that differentiate males and females of a species. Gender is more complex than this, however, because it includes social conceptions of what gender means, an individual's perception of his or her gender, and how he or she expresses it. For a long time, gender was conceived as a set of biologically derived traits.

More recently it is discussed more in terms of our social identity (see Topic 4.10). The biological view highlights the role of genetic influence and argues that differences will be both measurable and uncontrollable. Such differences include some aspects of cognition and skill proficiency. However, this is not a complete explanation, and evidence to support it has been limited. Similarly, researchers have looked for evidence of specific male/female differences in domains such as motor skills, language use, and intelligence. Such studies have proved inconclusive.

Critical social psychologists would argue that people using phrases like "boys will be boys" is an example of gender socialization.

In contrast to these lines of inquiry, the social identity approach suggests that gender is shaped by the transmission of norms, values, expected behaviors, and so on. Such gender schemas, it is argued, influence our behavior to a far greater extent than biology. Owing to this tension between biological and social influences, gender can be see as a key area in the nature/ nurture debate (see Topic 1.10).

The Genderbread person

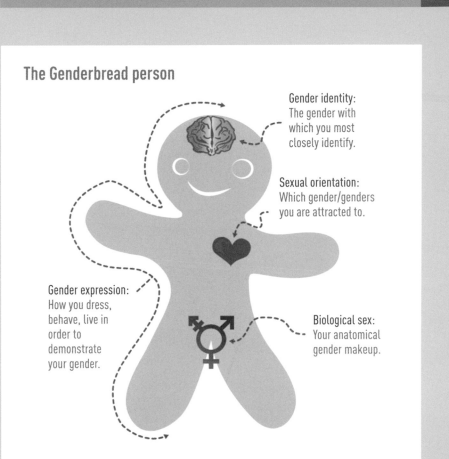

Gender identity:
The gender with which you most closely identify.

Sexual orientation:
Which gender/genders you are attracted to.

Gender expression:
How you dress, behave, live in order to demonstrate your gender.

Biological sex:
Your anatomical gender makeup.

Sam Killerman's Genderbread person reflects the complexity of trying to explain gender and sexuality. In addition to—sometimes in spite of—our anatomical makeup, we must also consider the gender with which we most closely identify and the gender(s) to which we are attracted.

8.10 Psychopathology

At what point does someone's difficulty in forming relationships become a personality disorder?

The assumption that any given characteristic is normally distributed (see Topic 8.2) means that people at the extremes of the distribution are, statistically, exceptional and have either, for example, very high or very low intelligence. There are only a few of them.

A key issue concerns the point at which an individual makes the transition from this extreme to **psychopathology**. For example, when does someone's low mood become a cause for real concern?

On the one hand clinicians and educationalists seek to assess the person compared to his/her peers. On the other hand they need to judge whether the characteristics being observed meet the criteria for psychopathology, a process heavily dependent on current theories of the condition.

Tests play a major role, here. The Minnesota Multiphasic Personality Inventory is a comprehensive test of personality and psychopathology and covers such areas as antisocial behavior, suicidal-death ideation, shyness, and psychotic tendencies. Other tests are more targeted.

While there is no doubt that the gray area between normality, exceptionality, and psychopathology is difficult to navigate, problems are being addressed with increasingly sophisticated assessment tools and advances in theory.

Disorders such as psychosis and depression have been reported since antiquity.

Exceptionality

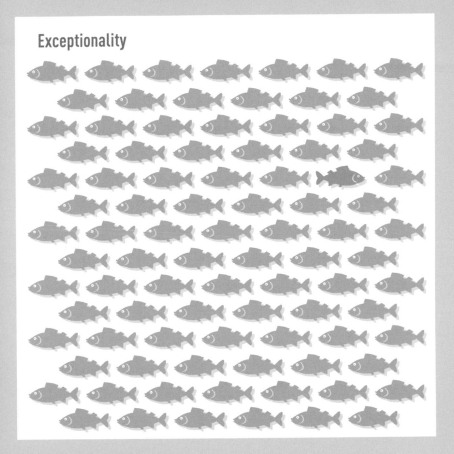

Swimming against the flow gets one noticed but whether the outcome is positive or negative depends on the reasons for being different. It could, for example, be because of an exceptional talent or because of a disabling psychological condition such as schizophrenia.

MENTAL HEALTH

Many people will live their entire lives without experiencing, or being affected by, mental health problems. However a significant percentage will not.

It is estimated that between 18–36% of people will experience some form of mental health difficulty throughout their lifetime, with one in four families estimated to contain a member with mental health problems. Some conditions, such as psychosis, are short-lived or sporadic in nature while others—personality disorders, for example—are more stable. Some mental health problems are more likely to affect us at specific points in our lives—degenerative disorders, for example, or stress.

Typically, diagnosis of a mental disorder depends on the identification of a particular set of symptoms, often under a given set of circumstances. These classifications are outlined in a variety of diagnostic manuals. One

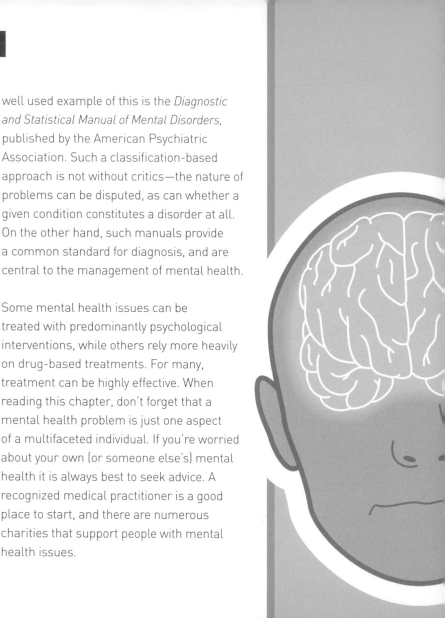

well used example of this is the *Diagnostic and Statistical Manual of Mental Disorders*, published by the American Psychiatric Association. Such a classification-based approach is not without critics—the nature of problems can be disputed, as can whether a given condition constitutes a disorder at all. On the other hand, such manuals provide a common standard for diagnosis, and are central to the management of mental health.

Some mental health issues can be treated with predominantly psychological interventions, while others rely more heavily on drug-based treatments. For many, treatment can be highly effective. When reading this chapter, don't forget that a mental health problem is just one aspect of a multifaceted individual. If you're worried about your own (or someone else's) mental health it is always best to seek advice. A recognized medical practitioner is a good place to start, and there are numerous charities that support people with mental health issues.

Contents

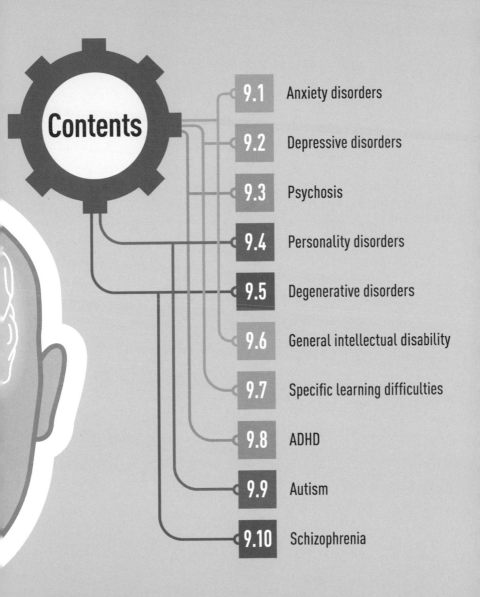

9.1 Anxiety disorders

9.2 Depressive disorders

9.3 Psychosis

9.4 Personality disorders

9.5 Degenerative disorders

9.6 General intellectual disability

9.7 Specific learning difficulties

9.8 ADHD

9.9 Autism

9.10 Schizophrenia

9.1 Anxiety disorders

Anxiety disorders are wide ranging. Many people respond well to talking therapies, such as cognitive behavioral therapy (CBT).

Anxiety disorders include obsessive-compulsive disorder (OCD), phobias, panic disorder, generalized anxiety disorder (GAD), and post-traumatic stress disorder (PTSD).

- OCD revolves around obsessions and compulsions that distress the sufferer or disproportionately consume his or her time. This can lead to cautious or ritualistic behaviors.

- Phobias involve a problematic fear that is out of proportion to the danger posed. These include agoraphobia, social phobias, and phobias linked to specific targets.

- Panic disorders involve panic attacks, which include physical symptoms and changes in behavior that seek to avoid situations that might provoke an attack. Onset is generally late teens and it is more common among females.

- GAD is characterized by acute anxiety with no specific trigger, but that occurs most days for six months or more.

- PTSD can result from a traumatic event. Symptoms include avoidance of reminders of the event, reliving the experience, and increased arousal (including insomnia).

Phobias are varied. *Gnosiophobia* is a fear of knowledge, *peladophobia*, a fear of bald people.

For most anxiety-based disorders, CBT can be an effective tool. However, for some (OCD, PTSD) it has limited success in some cases, and can be supplemented with pharmacological treatments.

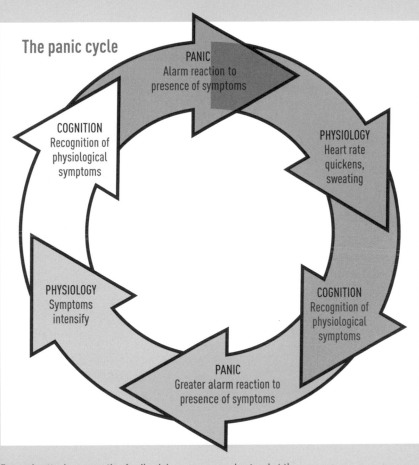

The panic cycle

PANIC
Alarm reaction to
presence of symptoms

PHYSIOLOGY
Heart rate
quickens,
sweating

COGNITION
Recognition of
physiological
symptoms

COGNITION
Recognition of
physiological
symptoms

PHYSIOLOGY
Symptoms
intensify

PANIC
Greater alarm reaction to
presence of symptoms

For panic attacks, a negative feedback loop can occur due to what the psychologist Clark referred to as a catastrophic misinterpretation of one's own symptoms.

9.2 Depressive disorders

The causes of depression may be biological, developmental, or social.

Broadly speaking, a "major" depressive disorder is diagnosed when five symptoms are observed in the same two-week period. The symptoms can be any five from a list that includes being in a depressed mode most of the day, significant weight loss, regular insomnia, fatigue, feelings of guilt or worthlessness, and a diminished ability to think.

Depression may arise from one of three causes. Biological causes include low levels of neurotransmitters, such as serotonin, noradrenaline, and dopamine. Developmental causes include learnt distortions in cognition and learned helplessness. Social causes might include a history of child abuse or current social isolation.

Studies looking at prevalence across different countries suggests around three to seven percent of people are diagnosed with depression at some point in their lives. Of these, some 10 to 20 percent may later develop bipolar disorders featuring episodes of mania. Typical onset of depression is around 20 to 30 years of age. Suicide rates for people with depression are high at around 15 percent.

According to the CDC, depression is the most common type of mental illness in the U.S.

Effective treatment usually involves a combination of drugs that act on neurotransmitters and talking therapies, such as CBT. For some forms of depression, there is some evidence that electroconvulsive therapy can be effective.

Symptoms of depression

Behavioral symptoms include withdrawal from others; neglecting responsibilities; being agitated or unable to settle; increased alcohol consumption.

Thought-related symptoms include frequent self-criticism; impaired concentration; confusion; and indecision.

Emotional symptoms include sadness; anxiety; mood swings; lack of confidence; irritability.

Physical symptoms include chronic fatigue; lack of energy; sleeping too much or too little; weight gain or loss; muscle pain.

People frequently dismiss symptoms of depression because they are often inconspicuous—it is not unusual to feel tired, low, or achy, for example. This makes depression difficult to diagnose.

9.3 Psychosis

Psychosis is a condition in which people experience a state of mind that leads them to lose contact with reality.

Symptoms of a psychotic episode include hallucinations; paranoid delusions or bizarre beliefs; *catatonia*; intense but purposeless movement, such as walking in fast circles; and not engaging with anything else. Thought disorders, in which a person's thoughts become intensely disturbed and disorganized, can also be a sign of psychosis.

Psychosis is seen in severe cases of depression, disorders such as schizophrenia (see Topics 9.2 and 9.10), and numerous other disorders (see opposite). It is also linked with other conditions, such as neurodegenerative disorders including Alzheimer's and Parkinson's (see Topic 9.5) and poisoning. This is sometimes called secondary psychosis.

Some psychologists have challenged the concept of psychosis. They argue that some symptoms—for example, internal voices and monologue—are highly common in those considered "normal." They suggest that interpretation by both the individual and clinician causes these symptoms to point to a disorder.

Treatment is specific to the conditions linked to psychosis, but typically involve drug regimes. These can be effective, but can also have significant side effects. Early intervention improves outcomes.

Hallucinations are not always psychotic. Those experienced while half asleep, for example, are normal and common.

Delusional episodes

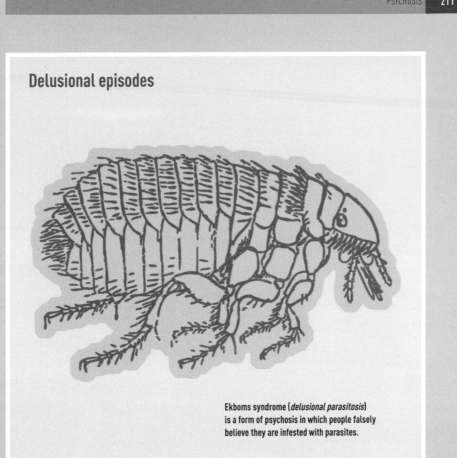

Ekboms syndrome (*delusional parasitosis*)
is a form of psychosis in which people falsely
believe they are infested with parasites.

Psychosis comes in many forms. In sufferers of Ekboms syndrome,
delusions can be so strong that individuals cannot grasp the lack of
real infestation and reject treatment for their psychological condition.

9.4 Personality disorders

People with personality disorders do not always recognize that there is a problem. This can make them difficult to treat.

An individual can be diagnosed as having a personality disorder (PD) if he or she betrays pathological personality traits (see Topic 8.3) and is unable to function socially.

A PD is confirmed if these impairments are stable over time, unusual for the individual stage of development or environment, and not due to physical injury or drugs.

Specific personality disorders can be identified by examining a variety of traits. Antisocial personality disorder, for example, is characterized by low anxiety and high levels of hostility, among other traits. Those suffering from borderline personality disorder, however, show high levels of both these traits.

Overall prevalence of personality disorders is around six to ten percent, with prevalence of common disorders (schizotypal, antisocial, borderline, histrionic) around two to three percent. Little work conclusively identifies the causes of PD, although childhood abuse and neglect are often implicated.

Not all researchers agree that there is such a thing as a "normal" personality, from which personality disorders are distinct.

PD treatment is a controversial subject and a challenging area. This is because PDs are stable and hard to affect. However, attempts to treat them typically involve talking therapies including psychotherapy, family therapy, and group therapy.

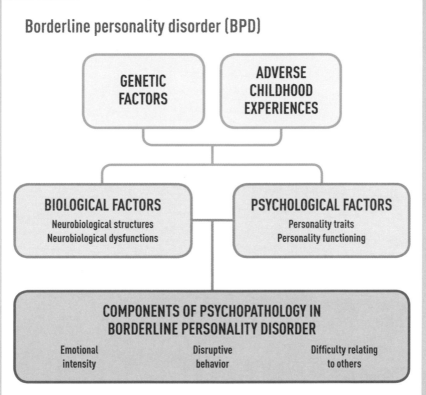

Borderline personality disorder (BPD)

GENETIC FACTORS

ADVERSE CHILDHOOD EXPERIENCES

BIOLOGICAL FACTORS
Neurobiological structures
Neurobiological dysfunctions

PSYCHOLOGICAL FACTORS
Personality traits
Personality functioning

COMPONENTS OF PSYCHOPATHOLOGY IN BORDERLINE PERSONALITY DISORDER

Emotional intensity

Disruptive behavior

Difficulty relating to others

The biopsychosocial model of borderline personality disorder (Leichsenring and colleagues, 2011).

This model argues that BPD is influenced by a combination of genetic and early environmental factors, which interact with biological factors and psychosocial traits. Various behavioral symptoms result.

9.5 Degenerative disorders

Some disorders of the brain result from progressive deterioration at the neural level. Many are characterized by cognitive decline and some with aging.

Degenerative disorders include dementia, Parkinson's disease, and multiple sclerosis (MS). Here are some of the most prevalent examples:

- Dementia is an umbrella term that refers to age-related cognitive decline. Prevalence is about seven percent in 65 years and over; 30 percent in 85 years and over. Alzheimer's disease is the most common form, caused by the development of neural and chemical abnormalities, which leads to cell death. It primarily affects the cortex. Intellectual decline is progressive and affects memory, language, executive function (see Topic 5.5), and personality.

- Parkinson's disease is a progressive neurological condition, starting in the basal ganglia (see Topic 2.2). It affects movement primarily. Prevalence is estimated at 1 in 500, with onset usually at 50 years and over. Men are slightly more affected than women. The characteristic symptoms are motor—tremor, stiffness, slowness. Some 70 percent go on to develop dementia and cognitive deterioration.

- MS refers to a progressive deterioration of the myelin sheath that insulates neurons throughout the brain and spinal cord. Prevalence is less than 1 in 500, with onset between 20 to 40 years. MS is more common in women and in white people. It affects motor, perceptual, cognitive, and emotional functions. Life expectancy is reduced.

The boxer Muhammad Ali contracted Parkinson's disease in his forties, probably as a result of repetitive concussion.

Alzheimer's

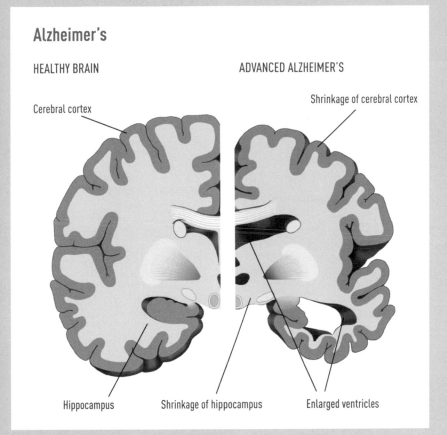

HEALTHY BRAIN

ADVANCED ALZHEIMER'S

Cerebral cortex

Shrinkage of cerebral cortex

Hippocampus

Shrinkage of hippocampus

Enlarged ventricles

A comparison of a healthy brain and one in the advanced stages of
Alzheimer's show the effects of massive cell death on brain size.

9.6 General intellectual disability

Having a low IQ has a significant impact on the ability to master basic life skills, such as using public transportation.

General intelligence (see Topic 8.4), as measured using IQ tests, is a criterion of general intellectual disability (GID). People with IQs above 130 or below 75 are equally exceptional. The former are considered exceptionally able, the latter intellectually disabled. Each group accounts for about three percent of the population.

Generally, individuals who fall into the low-IQ category have problems in the following three domains:

- Cognitively: They are affected in learning, memory, reasoning, and language.

- Socially: They have poor interpersonal skills, struggle to learn society's rules, and are socially naive.

- Practically: They are affected in basic life skills such as personal care; using transport, money, and telephones; and functioning at work.

Attitudes toward the intellectually disabled in antiquity were sometimes enlightened (Celts and Jews) and sometimes intolerant (Romans and Greeks).

The causes of GID are many and diverse. They might include any of the following: genetic abnormalities; intrauterine factors such as fetal alcohol levels; and perinatal and postnatal infections and injuries. As severity increases the causes become more identifiably specific and organic.

With all cases of GID, the level of support required corresponds to the severity of the condition.

Functioning with GID

SEVERITY	LEVEL OF FUNCTIONING
Mild IQ: 50–70 Mental age 9–12	Impairments not obvious; some educational achievement possible; generally capable of independent living; may be able to hold down a manual job.
Moderate IQ: 35–70 Mental age 6–9	Need supervision but within this can manage self care and carrying out a simple repetitive job. Need help with road sense and finances. Generally vulnerable so tend to live with parents or in residential care where supervision and help are available.
Severe/profound IQ: < 35 Mental age: < 6yrs	Cannot manage on their own; need highly structured lives with constant help but some self-care may be possible; language ability is absent or minimal; high prevalence of physical disability and immobility in the most profound cases.

With general intellectual disability, the degree of impairment in the cognitive, social, and practical domains depends on the degree of severity. This can be mild, moderate, or severe/profound.

9.7 Specific learning difficulties

A number of disorders target specific functions, making subjects like reading and mental arithmetic hard to grasp.

In contrast to general intellectual disability (see Topic 9.6), specific learning difficulties (SLDs) are limited in scope.

- Dyslexia is a specific problem with reading at the letter and word level. Other cognitive functions remain largely unaffected by the condition.

- Dyscalculia is specifically mathematical. It affects knowledge of mathematical symbols and operations involving these symbols.

Impairments with SLDs are diffuse, which means they can be diverse, which suggests they have diverse origins. This notion is supported by several observations. For example, people with dyslexia have an impaired working memory, and are also often quite disorganized and have problems remembering appointments. Furthermore, SLDs often co-occur and are sometimes **comorbid** with other conditions such as ADHD (see Topic 9.8). The picture that emerges is one in which the most salient problem, for example, math, is observed against a background of other problems.

SLDs are more prevalent in males than females and have a significant familial incidence. This suggests a genetic basis.

Consequently, in treating SLDs, research and clinical practice have increasingly focused on identifying the nature of the various component impairments rather than on the discrepancy between the person's general ability and his or her specific disability.

Comorbidity

Comorbidity is the rule, not the exception (Gilger and Kaplan, 2001).

DYSLEXIA

50% of children with dyslexia also meet the criterion of dyspraxia/developmental coordination disorder.

DYSPRAXIA

ADD/ADHD

25–40% of children with dyslexia also meet criteria for attention deficit hyperactivity disorder (ADHD).

DYSGRAPHIA

DYSCALCULIA

17–70% of children with dyslexia also meet the criteria for dyscalculia.

This diagram depicts the comorbidity of specific learning difficulties—where an individual may suffer from one or more of them. Estimates of overlap depend on the study. Some current estimates are listed above.

9.8 ADHD

A child displaying high levels of inattention and/or hyperactivity may have attention deficit hyperactivity disorder.

Attention deficit hyperactivity disorder (ADHD) is diagnosed in children whose inattention or hyperactivity impairs their development in the following ways.

■ Inattention includes symptoms such as being distracted; forgetful; and having trouble holding attention, including attending to details and organizing tasks and activities.

■ Hyperactivity issues include fidgeting; suddenly leaving one's seat; talking excessively; common interruptions; and being constantly on the go.

For a diagnosis to be made, several symptoms need to have been present prior to 12 years of age. Prevalence of ADHD is estimated to be around three to seven percent. There is some evidence of genetic causes.

Behavioral treatments for ADHD can include reinforcement of positive behaviors and non-reinforcement of negative ones (see Topic 6.2). Two common drug therapies are Ritalin and Dexedrine. These drugs are stimulants, but serve to reduce the need for external stimulation and thus calm the patient. Evidence suggests they are relatively safe. In the context of ADHD sufferers they bring neural function into line with that of so-called "normal" children. However, there are concerns that such drugs are being regularly prescribed to children who do not meet the diagnostic criteria.

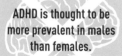

ADHD is thought to be more prevalent in males than females.

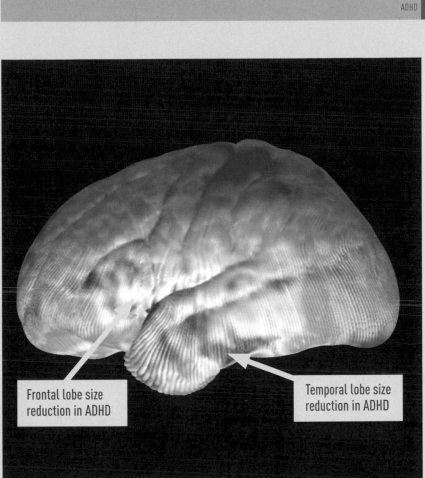

Frontal lobe size
reduction in ADHD

Temporal lobe size
reduction in ADHD

This color-coded image of the brain's left side shows the areas (red
and orange) that were smaller in children with attention disorders.

9.9 Autism

Individuals with autism find it hard to interact socially. They may also display poor language skills and repetitive behavior.

Typically, **autism** is first noticed in children from six months to three years of age, and affects one to two individuals per 1,000. It manifests in various ways and with increasing levels of severity. There are three major concerns.

The first is that people with autism have difficulty with social interaction. Secondly, they lack understanding and intuition about the thoughts and feelings of others, and reasons for behavior. Thirdly, when it comes to language, around 30 to 50 percent of people with autism lack the necessary skills with natural speech to manage day to day life. Repetitive behavior is also a feature of autism and includes:

- Stereotypy: repetitive hand flapping, body rocking.
- Repeatedly arranging items in a certain way.
- Engaging in ritualistic behavior.
- Focusing on a limited range of behaviors and self-injury.

Between 0.5 and 10 percent of autistic individuals have savant skills. These are superior abilities in domains such as perception or attention (see Topics 5.1 and 5.6).

Treatment takes the form of management, such as developing strategies to manage day-to-day situations; training to overcome deficits in specific skills sets; and reducing the effects of everyday stressors.

False links between autism and the MMR vaccine have been described as the most damaging hoax of the last 100 years.

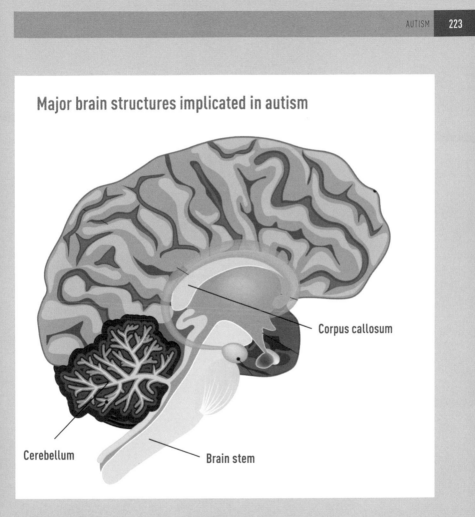

Major brain structures implicated in autism

Corpus callosum

Cerebellum

Brain stem

Like other psychological disorders, autism is likely to involve
numerous areas of the brain.

9.10 Schizophrenia

Having schizophrenia can often interfere with an individual's social or occupational function.

Schizophrenia is a mental disorder that is characterized by a variety of symptoms including delusions, hallucinations, and disorganized speech and behavior. It is diagnosed when an individual exhibits at least two of the prevailing symptoms for at least six months. The likelihood of an individual developing schizophrenia is around one percent.

It typically onsets between late adolescence and early adulthood. Research has identified genetic markers that are linked to increased susceptibility. Being related to someone with schizophrenia is also a risk factor. People with schizophrenia may also have non-genetic neurological differences. For example, neurotransmitter production and uptake may differ. Some evidence also points to interaction between biological factors and environmental stress.

Treatment for the disorder often revolves around antipsychotic drugs. Although frequently effective, these have multiple negative side effects. Drug regimes can be combined with psychological interventions.

Outcomes are varied: 20 percent of patients will only have one acute episode; 33 percent will have several episodes but generally improve; around 10 percent will not achieve the same level of functioning they had prior to diagnosis.

Schizophrenia symptoms are rarely constant. Rather they undulate, becoming more or less severe.

Schizophrenia is regularly poorly depicted in films and other media. For example, multiple personalities are not a defining characteristic of schizophrenia. This disorder can be a lonely experience, sometimes presenting a distorted view of the world that can be confusing and scary.

APPLICATIONS & GUIDANCE

10

P sychology is, at its heart, what we call an applied discipline. From the very beginning, practitioners have used the insights psychology produces in incredibly diverse ways. These include trying to improve people's' lives in terms of psychological health; making organizations function more effectively; and making processes more fair.

Sometimes the interventions are small. Perhaps a psychologist will suggest a new way of selecting individuals for an occupation, for example. At other times, intervention may be of historical importance—say, through a psychologist influencing public policy on issues such as the racial desegregation of schools.

No ten topics could come close to covering fully the range of activities psychology has been applied in, so we have chosen a selection that includes mental health (counseling, clinical psychology, child assessment and

Continues overleaf

intervention); organizational psychology (personnel selection and leadership); the legal system (jury decision-making, eye-witness memory); and those concerned with wider social issues (contact theory and minority influence).

Beyond the areas covered in this chapter, almost every aspect of human functioning has been impacted by psychology one way or another. Here are a few examples:

- Psychologists have contributed to solutions for human-computer system interaction and psychological ergonomics for airplane cockpits.
- Environmental psychologists have been involved in the configuration of housing estates to minimize crime.
- Educational psychologists have developed ways of teaching effectively in the classroom.

These are just some of the ways in which psychological intervention and guidance come to the fore.

Contents

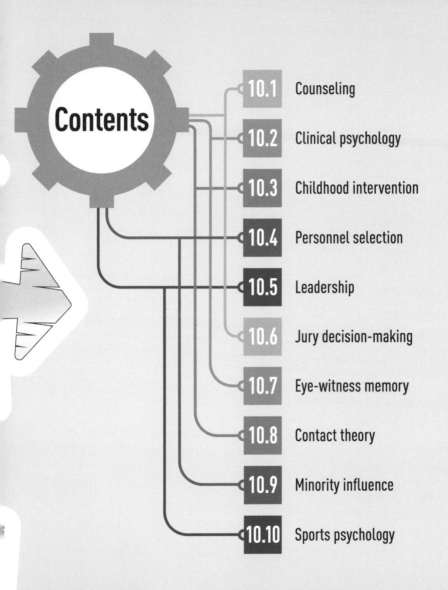

10.1 Counseling

10.2 Clinical psychology

10.3 Childhood intervention

10.4 Personnel selection

10.5 Leadership

10.6 Jury decision-making

10.7 Eye-witness memory

10.8 Contact theory

10.9 Minority influence

10.10 Sports psychology

10.1 Counseling

One-on-one counseling is an effective therapy for a wide range of psychological problems.

Counseling involves a professional relationship between a counselor and a client. Counselors help with a variety of psychological problems that fall within the following groups:

- Issues commonly faced by many people, such as bereavement, anxiety, relationship issues.

- Issues encountered more rarely, such as dealing with traumatic events or addictions.

- Highly individual issues—problems around unique sexual fetishes for example.

Counselors draw on one or more of the theoretical frameworks available to them. The process of counseling varies according to the approach. Thus, a cognitive behavioral approach may identify faulty thought patterns, test these against reality, and find ways of challenging them. In contrast, psychodynamic practitioners may use free association, discussion of dreams, and the identification of areas of tension. These can help to explore unconscious conflicts that may manifest in apparently unrelated psychological problems.

A 2004 survey by The American Psychological Association suggested that 50% of households in the US had a member seek mental health treatment in the previous 12 months.

Most forms of counseling are one-on-one, but group discussion can achieve similar results. No one approach is a cure-all, neither do any conclusively come out as being most effective in empirical studies. It is the differences between clients that make them more or less suitable.

What is involved?

CONFIDENTIAL
All conversations between an individual and his/her counselor are strictly confidential.

MAKING CHANGES
A counselor will advise on how to make changes to the current situation.

ASSESSMENT
A counselor will analyze and highlight specific needs.

LACK OF BIAS
Counselors are not there to make judgments.

UNDERSTANDING
Counseling helps an individual to make sense of his or her situation.

A GOOD EAR
One of the most important things is that a counselor is there to listen.

Counseling relies on talk-based therapies. Although one-on-one therapy is most common, it is not unusual for groups, couples or families to attend counseling sessions together.

10.2 Clinical psychology

Clinical psychologists may use specialist diagnostic tools when assessing mental health disorders.

Clinical psychologists work in large health organizations and in private practice, just as counselors do. As well as addressing the same issues as counselors (see Topic 10.1), clinical psychology considers more acute problems, such as neurological trauma, acute eating disorders, and criminal offender rehabilitation. Clinical psychologists are also more likely to serve in other roles, such as expert witnesses.

The main difference between the two disciplines is the level of qualification. Counseling is often based on experience rather than formal qualifications. Clinical psychologists, however, undertake formal doctoral level training. This includes research skills and the production of a thesis. They have access to, and expertise in, specialist diagnostic instruments, such executive function assessments, and so on (see Topic 5.5)

Although not licensed to prescribe medication, clinical psychologists may consider the use of drug therapies. This may be the case if seeking to reduce anxiety or manage sleep problems in order to stabilize a client before psychological treatment begins. However, clinical psychologists base their treatment on talking therapies, and use pharmacological options to a lesser extent than psychiatrists. Pyschiatrists take a more disease-based approach to mental health problems.

Clinical psychologists are expected to complete a thesis that presents new understanding in an area of their chosen subject.

Teamwork

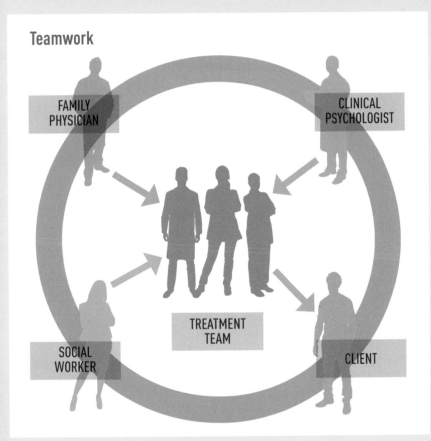

FAMILY PHYSICIAN

CLINICAL PSYCHOLOGIST

TREATMENT TEAM

SOCIAL WORKER

CLIENT

Clinical psychologists often work in multidisciplinary teams,
which may include family physicians, teachers, and social workers.
Clients may see these people one-on-one, too.

10.3 Childhood intervention

Sometimes, some children need a little more help in one or more areas of their development.

Educational assessments of a child's intellectual disability are based on a combination of IQ scores (see Topic 8.4) and specific skills. There are three general areas for concern:

■ Conceptual: language, reading, writing, math, reasoning.

■ Social: empathy, social judgment, interpersonal communication, and friendship management.

■ Practical: managing day-to-day activities.

Impairment can consist of a specific learning difficulty where only one area of function is impaired (dyslexia). Or it may be the result of internalizing disorders (anxiety/depression). It could also stem from externalizing disorders, such as attention-deficit disorder.

Impairment can also include issues with language and communication, including disorders such as autism and Asperger's syndrome. There may also be difficulty with sensory and physical issues (hearing/motor-control).

Intervention varies by diagnosis, and is tailored to each child. Typically they include an action plan with specific goals and methods (see opposite). They also vary in intensity. Whichever method is used, the interests and safey of the child and his/her impact on those around him/her are paramount.

Only in the fifth edition of the Diagnostic and Statistical Manual of Mental Disorders was "mental retardation" replaced with "intellectual disability."

A sample action plan

TARGET BEHAVIOR	SUCCESS CRITERIA	STRATEGIES AND SUPPORT	PROGRESS WITH PUPIL
To share with others	Shares favorite toys during free-play periods	Role modeling with teachers, siblings, and peers; positive reinforcement schedule (sticker chart)	Great progress: Has shared favorite toy for brief periods at playtime; has received nine sticker rewards
To be able to identify physical boundaries when interacting with others	No interventions of teachers due to physical altercations between pupil and other children	Use of interactive book series to explore social meanings of behavior Role plays of difficult/confusing interactions	Role modeling ok, but unwanted hugs have led to altercations with others; seems to be linked with recognition of ambiguous situations

This individual action plan is tailored to a child who has difficulty interacting socially. Plans are time-bound with monitoring arrangements. The plan identifies a number of behaviors for improvement, outlines specific strategies, and has space for keeping notes on outcomes.

10.4 Personnel selection

Are you well suited to your job? Perhaps you should take a personality test to find out . . .

Personnel selection was first addressed during World War I, when increasingly varied roles began to require different skills sets.

Nowadays, personnel assessors use various methods for matching suitability to task. These include questionnaires, interviews, or work-based assessments. To some extent, an employee's future performance can be predicted if the correct combination of mental-ability tests are combined with structured interviews or simulations of the role itself.

A popular instrument for measuring how people will operate in a workplace is the Myers-Briggs Type Indicator. (see opposite). The sixteen combinations produced are "types" that suggest how people will prefer to act in most situations.

Some researchers argue that employers should also ensure a candidate's personality fits the organization. Measures such as "openness to experience, conscientiousness, agreeableness, extroversion, and neuroticism" (OCEAN) are often used to achieve this.

The MBTI predicts how people will behave under high task demands.

However, although popular, these approaches are only half the story. Some suggest that, to ensure the best job/person fit, applicants should also be able to get to know the organization for which they are applying.

Myers-Briggs simplified

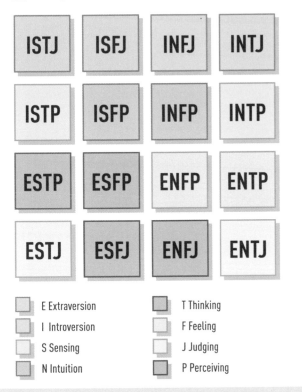

ISTJ ISFJ INFJ INTJ
ISTP ISFP INFP INTP
ESTP ESFP ENFP ENTP
ESTJ ESFJ ENFJ ENTJ

E Extraversion   T Thinking
I Introversion   F Feeling
S Sensing   J Judging
N Intuition   P Perceiving

The MBTI poses questions, the answers to which identify an individual's preferences for the above eight traits. The individual's personality is then further analyzed to assess which four of those traits most sum them up. The various combinations result in 16 personality types.

10.5 Leadership

What are the qualities of an effective leader? Much depends on situation and context.

Early accounts of leadership assumed that some people had particular characteristics that made them great leaders. They tried to identify these characteristics **empirically**, be they charisma, extroversion, or other traits.

Other theories focused on the particular behaviors that typify leadership, such as decisiveness. Neither approach has proved terribly successful in its attempt to understand the differences between a good leader and a bad one.

Alternative theories on leadership focus on situational factors. These approaches argue that sometimes a task-orientated leadership style is effective, but at other times a relationship-orientated style is important (see opposite). The former may involve supervising the work of others; the latter managing the interpersonal exchanges of others.

Similar to this, so-called transactional/transformational approaches suggest that a leader is effective to the extent that he or she can offer to achieve things that followers need or want.

Most recently, social identity approaches (see Topic 4.10) suggest that the concept of a good leader varies by context (for example in times of war vs. peace, prosperity vs. depression). Individuals perceived as both being representative of the group and meeting their goals at that point in time are more easily accepted.

New leaders possess idiosyncratic credit allowing them to break rules—for a while!

Leadership situations

Leader-member relations	Good	Good	Good
Task structure	High	High	Low
Position power	Strong	Weak	Strong
Favorableness of situation	Most favorable		
Appropriate leader behavior	Task-oriented		

Leader-member relations	Good	Poor	Poor
Task structure	Low	High	High
Position power	Weak	Strong	Weak
Favorableness of situation	Moderate favorable		
Appropriate leader behavior	Relationship-oriented		

Leader-member relations	Poor	Poor
Task structure	Low	Low
Position power	Strong	Weak
Favorableness of situation	Least favorable	
Appropriate leader behavior	Task-oriented	

Fielder's contingency theory argues that different tasks/people need different levels of situational control, and that these are best met through either task-orientated behaviors (low and high situational control) or relationship-orientated behaviors (medium control).

10.6 Jury decision-making

Are juries biased? They may not intend to be, but in certain circumstances, this seems to be the case.

Juries make decisions that can change lives. They display the same biases and benefits as other groups. Using mock juries in controlled cases, psychologists have also identified a number of specific biases. They include the following:

- Jurors tend to be more lenient toward people who are similar to them, say, in ethnicity or religion.

- They find attractive people guilty less often than unattractive ones.

- Jurors are less likely to find adults with child-like faces guilty of violent crimes, but more likely for crimes of negligence (Berry, Zebrowitz-McArthur 1988).

- Forepeople (often self-elected, white, well-educated males) have an undue influence. They use up to 35 percent of the speaking time and have a disproportionate impact on the verdict.

Alongside being less likely to be convicted, attractive people are more likely to succeed as litigants.

Work on procedural issues has generated a number of findings that could help to reduce possible biases. For example, polling publically during deliberation can create false local majorities, leading to conformity (see opposite and Topic 4.7). Likewise, six-person juries appear to be less representative than twelve-person juries. They involve less deliberation and have a slightly higher conviction rate.

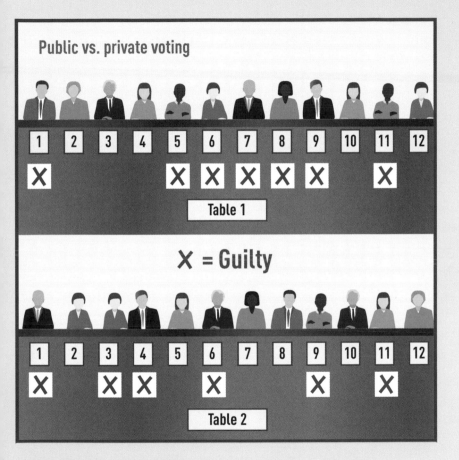

If juries poll in public sequentially (Table 1), chance can combine a minority of votes in one direction into a block. They can provide an apparent (but false) majority, and conformity can then bias the verdict. The answer? Private and/or simultaneous voting (Table 2).

10.7 Eye-witness memory

How accurately could you recall the events of an accident or incident that you have witnessed?

Eye-witness memory provides evidence for investigation teams and juries, but are they accurate? Pioneering work by researchers Yuille and Cutshall (1986) suggests that around 80 percent of the information given is true. However, important details such as hair color, height, weight, age, and clothing are often erroneous.

The way information is gained is important. Work by Loftus and Palmer (1974) shows interviewees questioned about a car accident. Asking whether a car in a video "contacted" or "smashed" into another, changed the perceived speed of the car from 31.8 mph (51.2 kph) to 40.5 mph (65.2 kph). Asking participants if they saw broken glass in the film (there was none) led them to report it more often if the car "smashed."

Psychologists have devised various techniques for improving eyewitness accounts. The Cognitive Interview (Geiselman, 1984) encourages interviewees to: state the context clearly; report everything (including apparently irrelevant information); engage in free recall; and repeat the account from the perspective of others. Enhanced versions of this model build rapport between interviewers and interviewees to reduce anxiety.

Enhanced cognitive interviews lead to more information and fewer inaccuracies being conveyed than free recall.

These measures maximize the activation of as many relevant memory traces as possible and evaluate them through repetition. As such they aim to improve accuracy.

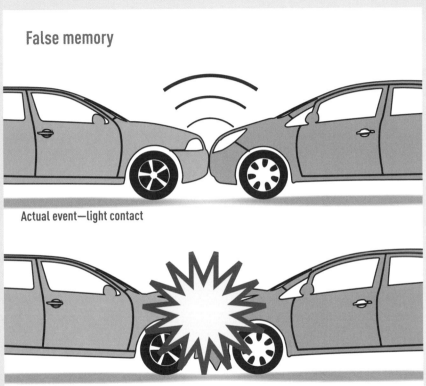

False memory

Actual event—light contact

False-memory event—head-on collision

Research on false memory effects suggest that small changes in the phrasing and form of questions can distort memory such that things that never happened are recalled.

10.8 Contact theory

Common biases are reduced—eliminated even—when two conflicting groups learn to work with one another.

While contact between conflicting groups can lead to escalation of tension, it is also one of the most powerful tools for reducing intergroup prejudice. Gordon Allport's contact theory (1954) argues that contact can reduce anxiety in intergroup situations. It also highlights similarities and reduces stereotypes (see Topic 4.3). Allport argues that four conditions must be met in any given situation:

- Equal status: Groups often have differing status in society. However, as long as equal status is maintained within the specific context, this condition can be met.

- Common goals: Activities that create common goals is beneficial. This could be as simple as a sports event in which teams are formed from members of both groups.

- Intergroup cooperation: This provides an opportunity for contact in which both parties are valued.

- Support from authority: Having the social or legal support of authorities is key. This changes social norms and helps ensure the other conditions are met.

Simply imagining contact with another group can be somewhat effective in reducing prejudice.

Other researchers have highlighted that optimal contact will not work immediately. Instead, success relies on frequent and prolonged contact. If these conditions are met, however, there will almost certainly be a reduction in prejudice between groups.

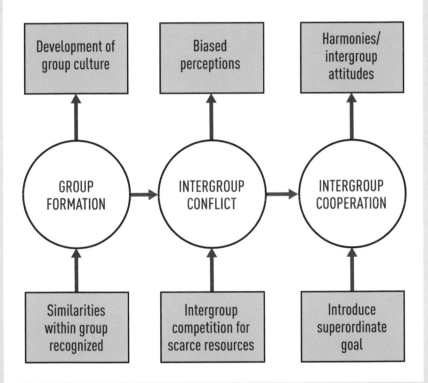

Realistic conflict theory

A diagrammatic look at Muzafer Sherif's Robbers cave study (1961) in which two groups of children visit summer camp. Each has a strong group identity and, initially, they compete over resources, leading to biased perceptions. Conflict shifts to harmony through numerous cooperative tasks.

10.9 Minority influence

Given the right conditions, it is possible for a minority group to influence the majority.

We know that majorities can make individuals conform (see Topic 4.7). We also know, however, that groups aren't static in their beliefs or behaviors. So how can minorities maximize on this to change opinion?

A social scientist named Serge Moscovici argued that minorities, rather than being passive recipients of influence, could also generate change (1969). He identified a number of attributes that make minorities effective.

In a task in which group members had to name the color of green slides of varying hue, accuracy was high—almost 100 percent. However, when two stooges were placed in the group, and answered "blue" to some of the trials, things changed. When the stooges were inconsistent, the accuracy of the remaining group members remained high. However, when the two stooges consistently named the slides blue, accuracy of the group fell by almost ten percent. Moscovici concluded that consistency is a key behavioral style for minorities to adopt. He also identified that minorities need to be seen to be acting fairly, to have autonomy, to be invested in the process, and to be flexible.

Moscovici's ideas help us understand the historical successes and failures of minority influence.

It is interesting to note that minority influence is not always recognized explicitly: Social cryptoamnesia is a phenomena in which an attitude is changed, but the source forgotten, leading to the belief that one came to the viewpoint oneself...

Green or blue?

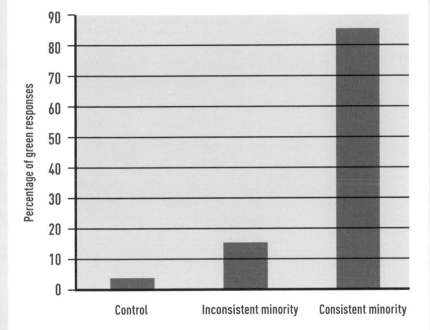

Serge Moscovici's green/blue experiment is an interesting comparison to Asch's line judgment task (see page 99). Here, just as there, people conform to the judgments of those who are quite clearly wrong.

10.10 Sports psychology

A sports person's mental state is just as important as his or her physical state, perhaps even more so.

Sports psychology encompasses cognitive psychology, social psychology, and individual differences (see Topic 8.1). It may also rely on biomechanics and kinesiology (the study of human movement).

Methods may include training in an environment similar to that of one's performance. This makes behaviors more hard-wired and means that other factors, such as anxiety or high arousal, affect performers less. Such measures could involve physically experiencing the environment—for example training with crowd noise—or through visualization.

Sports psychologists may also counsel coaches, in order to encourage training that fosters internal motivation and effort. They may also develop exercises that enhance mental toughness, or use CBT-type techniques to help conquer loss of confidence.

Other areas that fall within the scope of sports psychology include improved engagement among the wider public, increased understanding of team dynamics, and helping athletes recover from injuries.

Sports psychology can trace its roots to psychological training regimes among ancient Greek athletes.

There is no doubt that competitors with a high degree of motor skill benefit from managing motivation and anxiety. They also seek to maximize a sense of flow, and minimize variation in behavior. In many cases, sports psychology can provide the edge needed to win.

Developing a plan

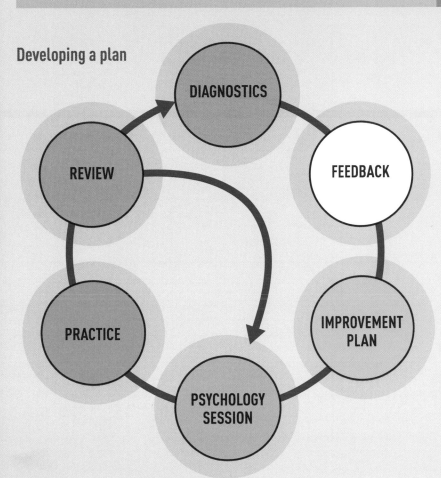

When you have a single chance to leverage months or years of training to deliver your best performance, the psychological preparation you have made can be the difference between success and failure.

Glossary

Behaviorism

An approach to psychology that assumes behaviors are learnt through a combination of rewards (positive reinforcement) and punishments (negative reinforcement) in response to a stimuli or behavior. This approach does not take much account of the role of information processing (See Cognition, below) on behavior.

Biopsychology

An approach to psychology rooted in the biology of the body, looking at issues such as the physiology of the nervous system, the functioning of hormones, and inherited traits.

Cognition

The act of processing information. The term is often used to refer to the suite of mental abilities related to "higher" thought processes such as reasoning, memory, problem solving, decision making, and the use of language.

Cognitive behavioral therapy (CBT)

A powerful psychological therapy that relies on talking to help people identify erroneous beliefs and to modify aspects of a subject's cognition processes in order to change behavior. CBT can be used to treat disorders such as anxiety (and more serious mental health problems).

Comorbid

Relating to a psychological or medical condition that often occurs in association with another one. The comorbid condition can also occur independently, and rates of comorbidity between X and Y can differ from those between Y and X. For example, disorder X may almost always be accompanied by Y, but Y may often occur without the presence of X.

Empirical

An approach to knowledge in which experience, observation, and experiment are taken as the basis for understanding. Theories are developed in order to explain empirical evidence, and fail when confronted by evidence disputing their predictions.

Gestalt

From a German word meaning a group or form, gestalt psychology is an approach to understanding the operation of mind by viewing it as a global whole distinct from its individual component parts.

Heuristic

A cognitive shortcut that saves mental effort in a thought process but may be less accurate. For example, believing that information from a trusted celebrity will be accurate. Heuristics are often relied on when people are under high pressure or are not motivated to be accurate.

Modularity

The concept that the mind is composed of separate modules that have evolved semi-independently to fulfill distinct roles. These can be physical (certain areas of the brain linked to speech) or functional (short-term memory).

Motor control

The means by which the central nervous system (CNS) controls and coordinates the motion of muscles and the body as a whole through a mixture of conscious and subconscious mechanisms.

Neuron

A type of cell found in the brain and wider nervous system, capable of receiving, processing, and transmitting electrical and chemical signals to others through connections known as synapses. The human brain is thought to contain 86 billion neurons.

Neurotransmitters

Any one of several dozen chemicals in the body that are used to transmit signals between neurons. They can also affect muscle and gland cells and influence the function of the rest of the organism.

Nomothetic

An approach to psychology in which the individual is principally understood by reference to the behavior of larger groups and more generalized norms. For example, understanding a person's level of extroversion by comparing them to the population mean on a questionnaire.

Syndrome

A collection of symptoms that appear together and may be evidence of an underlying disease or disorder.

Index

ability emotional intelligence 192
accident, responding to an 97
ADHD (attention deficit hyperactivity disorder) 218, 219, 220–1
adrenal gland 50
adrenaline 162, 163
aging 80–1
agnosia 48
Allport, Gordon 244
Alzheimer's disease 210, 214, 215
American Psychological Association 24, 230
Ames Room 111
amnesia 26, 28, 46, 48, 114, 122
analogy, problem solving by 134
anger 168–9
antisocial personality disorder 212
anxiety disorders 206–7
aphasia 48
aptitudes, intellectual 190–1
Asch, Solomon 88, 98, 99, 247
Asperger's syndrome 234
associative learning 40
associative stage
  and skill acquisition 148, 151
attachment theory 158
attention
  focused 26
  selective and divided 120–1
attention deficit hyperactivity disorder
  see ADHD
attitude formation 30, 86–7
attribution making 88, 94–5, 196
auditory channel 120
auditory filter model 120, 121
autism 76, 136, 137, 222–3, 234
automated system 118
automatic responses 30, 31

automatic stage
  and skill acquisition 148, 151
autonomic system 42
availability heuristic 126
axon 44, 45

Baddeley, Alan 122
balance theory 87
Bandura, Albert 138
Bargh, John 30
basal ganglia 40, 214
Baumeister, Roy 166
Bayley Scale of Infant Development 72
behavior
  and evolution 54–5
  and genes 52–3
  and hormones 50–1
behavioral psychologists 56
behaviorism/behaviorists 14, 28, 32, 250
bell-shaped curve 185
biases 94, 194
  in decision-making 126
  and juries 240
Big Five 186, 187, 192
Binet-Simon Intelligence Test 72
biological determinism 32
biological influences 35–57
biopsychology 190, 250
birth defects 62–3
borderline personality disorder (BPD) 212, 213
brain 26, 42, 54
  anatomy of 40–1
  and autism 223
  cortical lobes and functions of 41
  memory processing 46, 116
  and phrenology 38, 39
  plasticity of 64–5

scanning of 18, 38
structure of the mind 66–7
  see also neuropsychology
brain damage 26, 28, 64, 190
  effects of 48–9
brainstem 40
British Psychology Society 24
Broadbent, Donald 120
Broca, Paul 38
bystander helping 96–7

Carney, Dana 88
Cattell, Raymond 186, 187
cell assemblies 46–7
central nervous system (CNS) 42, 43
cerebral cortex 40, 41, 54
childhood intervention 234–5
children and infants
  and ADHD 220–1
  forming friendships 78–9
  and language learning 146
  measuring intelligence 72
  mother-infant bond 56
  and self-recognition 74–5
  testing of 70–1
  theory of mind 76–7
choice 126–7
Chomsky, Noam 146
classical conditioning 142, 144–5
clinical psychology 232–3
codes of conduct 24
cognition 107–29, 250
  need for (NFC) 194–5
  social 76
cognitive algebraic models 88, 89
cognitive approach 14
cognitive behavioral therapy (CBT) 168, 169, 208, 250

cognitive development 68
Cognitive Interview 242
cognitive learning 140–1
cognitive stage
   and skill acquisition 148, 151
collectivism 197
comorbid/comorbidity 218, 219, 250
comparative psychology 56–7
complex motivation 160–1
concept maps 141
conditioning, classical 142, 144–5
configural processing 113
conformity 98–9, 246
consciousness 28–9, 30
consolidation 116
contact theory 244–5
contingency theory 239
continuity 68–9
correlational methods 20
correspondence inference theory 95
cost-reward model 96
counseling 230–1
covariation models 94
cultural dimensions theory 197
cultural influences 196–7

decision-making 126–7
   jury 240–1
declarative/nondeclarative memory
   114, 115
deductive reasoning 128
degenerative disorders 80, 210, 214–15
delusional episodes 211
dementia 80, 214
depression 208–9, 234
developmental psychology 59–81
dimensional approach 182
disciplinary convergence 18–19
discontinuity 68–9
discourse analysis 22
distress 162
divided attention 120–1
domain generality 66, 67
domain specificity 66, 152
dopamine 44

doughnut deliberations 31
dual-process models 30–1
Duchenne smile 172, 173
dyscalculia 218, 219
dysgraphia 219
dyslexia 218, 219
dyspraxia 219

ego depletion 166–7
Einstein, Albert 152, 182
elaboration likelihood model (ELM)
   92, 93
embarrassment 170
emotional intelligence 192–3
emotions, perception of 193
encoding 116
environmental dependency syndrome 118
Ericsson, Anders 152
estrogen 50
ethics 24–5
evolution
   and behavior 54–5
evolutionary psychology 32
executive function 26, 114, 118–19
expectancy 160, 161
experimental method 20
expertise acquisition 152–3
explicit learning 86
eye-witness memory 242–3

face recognition 112–13
false-belief test 76, 77
false memory 243
Fernandez, Ephrem 168
fetal alcohol syndrome 62
fight-or-flight response 50, 54, 162
Fitts-Anderson model 148
flow 172
focus groups 23
focused attention 26
Foot, Philippa 176
footbridge dilemma 176, 177
forgiveness, seeking 171
Freud, Sigmund 29
friendships, forming 78–9

Gardner, Howard 190, 191
gender 198–9
   stereotypes 91
Genderbread person 199
General Factor of Personality 186, 187, 192
general intellectual disability (GID)
   216–17
general intelligence 188–9, 190
General Problem Solver computer
   program 134
generalized anxiety disorder (GAD) 206
genes/genetics 32, 33, 198
   and behavior 52–3
   definition 52
   and gender 198
   and schizophrenia 53
genotype 52
Gestalt 18, 110, 251
grammar 124, 142
grounded theory 22, 23
group membership 90, 104
groups
   reducing of intergroup prejudice 244
guilt 170–1
Gupta, Usha 174

habituation 70
hallucinations 210
happiness 172–3
Harlow, Harry 56
Hatfeld, Elaine 174
Hebb, Donald 46
Heider, Fritz 87
Heine, Steven 196
Heinrich, Joe 196
Helsinki Declaration 25
hemispherectomy 64
herd psychology 182
heuristic-systematic model (HSM) 92
heuristic(s) 194, 251
   availability 126
   representative 126
hippocampus 46, 116
Hitch, Graham 122
hobbits and orcs problem 135

homunculus 119
hormones 50–1
Hubel, David 110
hyperactivity 220
hypothalamus 162
hypothesis testing 140

identity
  group 104
  self- 104, 105
  social 104–5, 198, 238
idiographic method 182
implicit learning 86, 142–3
implicit processing 30
impression formation 88–9
individual differences 182–3
individualism 197
inductive reasoning 128
infants see children and infants
ingroups 104
insight, problem solving by 134
Institutional Review Board (IRB) 24
instrumental learning 134, 136–7
instrumentality 160, 161
intellectual aptitudes 190–1
intelligence(s) 80
  emotional 192–3
  fluid or crystallized 80
  general 188–9, 190
  general intellectual disability (GID)
    216–17
  measuring of 72–3, 188
  multiple 190–1
IQ (intelligence quotient) 188, 189,
  216, 234

joy 172–3
judgment 126–7
jury decision-making 240–1

Kahneman, Daniel 126, 127
Katz, Daniel 86
Kelley, Harold 94
Killerman, Sam 199
Kobayash, Emiko 170

language 18, 26, 54
  learning 146–7
  skills 124–5
leadership 238–9
learning 56, 131–51
  cognitive 140–1
  explicit 86
  implicit 86, 142–3
  instrumental 134, 136–7
  of language 146–7
  observational 138–9
  practice and long-term 150
  skills 148–9
learning curves 150, 151
learning difficulties, specific (SLDs)
  218–19, 234
life-span psychology 59–81
limbic system 40
long-term potentiation 46
Lorenz, Konrad 56
love 174–5

Markus, Hazel 196
Marr, David 18, 112
marriage 174
Maslow, Abraham 158–9
means-end analysis 134
memory(ies) 26
  and cell assemblies 46–7
  consolidation of a 116
  declarative 114, 115
  eye-witness 242–3
  false 243
  long-term 114, 115, 116
  nondeclarative 114, 115
  processes 115–17
  prospective 114
  recall 116, 117
  short-term 114, 116
  systems 114–15
  working 122–3
  see also amnesia
mental health 203–25
Milgram experiments 100–1, 251
mind

modularity of 26–7, 38, 48, 66
  structure 66–7
  theory of 76–7
Minnesota Multiphasic Personality
  Inventory 200
minority influence 246–7
mirror drawing 143
modularity 26–7, 38, 48, 66, 251
moral dilemmas 176–7
Moscovici, Serge 246, 247
mother-infant bond 56
motivation, complex 160–1
motor control 40, 251
Mullen Scales of Early Learning 72
multidisciplinary approach 18–19
multiple intelligences 190–1
multiple sclerosis (MS) 214
Myers-Briggs Type Indicator 236, 237

nature/nurture debate 32–3, 198
need for cognition (NFC) 194–5
needs, hierarchy of 158–9
nervous system 42–3, 44–5
neurons 42, 44–5, 46, 251
neuropsychology 28, 38–9, 48, 110
neurotransmitters 44–5, 174, 208, 251
Newell, Allen 134
Nim Chimpsky 147
nomothetic 182, 251
Norenzayan, Ara 196
Norman, Donald 118
Nuremberg trials (1945-46) 25

obedience, acts of 100–1
object recognition 18, 112
observational learning 138–9
obsessive-compulsive disorder (OCD) 206
OCEAN 236
older, getting 80–1
outgroups 104

panic disorders 206, 207
parasympathetic system 42
Parkinson's disease 210, 214
Pavlov, Ivan 144, 145

peer interactions 78
Penfield, Wilder 38, 46
perception 26, 110–11
  of emotions 193
peripheral nervous system (PNS) 42, 43
personality disorders 212–13
personality tests 236–7
personality traits 186–7, 192, 194
personnel selection 182, 184, 236–7
persuasion 30
  and need for cognition 195
persuasion susceptibility 92–3, 194
phenomenological consciousness 28
phenotype 52
phobias 144, 206
phonological loop 122
phrenology/phrenologists 38, 39
Piaget, Jean 68
positive psychology 158, 172
positivism 22
Posner, Michael 120
post-traumatic stress disorder (PTSD) 206
postmodern perspectives 22
practice 148, 150–1
preferential looking 70
problem-solving 134–5
progesterone 50
psychological testing 184–5
psychology, definition 14
psychopathology 200–1
psychosis 210–11

Q-sort 182, 183
qualitative methods 22–3
quantitative methods 20–1, 22

Raven's Progressive Matrices 188, 189
realist conflict theory 245
reasoning 128–9
  deductive 128
  inductive 128
  scientific 128
recognition, object and face 112–13
reflective responses 30, 31
representative heuristic 126

Rorschach inkblot test 15
rouge removal test 74, 75
Rousseau, Jean-Jacques 68
rules of thumb 126

Sally-Anne task 76, 77
savants 190, 222
schizophrenia 201, 210, 224–5
  and genes 53, 224
scientific approach 16–17
scientific reasoning 128
selective attention 120–1
selective auditory attention 120
selective visual attention 120
self-actualization 158, 159
self-categorization theory 104
self-control 166
self-identity 104, 105
self-recognition 74–5
self-referential approach 182, 183
Seligman, Martin 172
Shallice, Tim 118
shame 170
Sherif, Muzafer 98, 245
Simon, Herbert 134
Singh, Pushpa 174
single-case methodology 182
skill learning 148–9, 150, 151
skill types 149
Skinner, B.F. 56, 136
smiling 172, 173
social behavior 83–105
social cognition 76
social cryptoamnesia 246
social facilitation 102–3
social identity 104–5, 198, 238
social loafing 102–3
socialization 198
Spearman, Charles 188
specific learning difficulties (SLDs)
  218–19, 234
speech production, stages of 124, 125
sports psychology 248–9
Stereotype Content model 90
stereotypes 30, 88, 126, 194, 244

formation 90–1
  gender 91
stress
  appraising 164–5
  coping strategies 164
  defining 162–3
  positive and negative 162, 164
suicide 208
sympathetic system 42
syndromes 48, 251

Tajfel, Henri 104
talking therapies 232
teratogens 62
testing infants 70–1
Thorndike, Edward 136
token economies 136, 137
track dilemma 176, 177
trait emotional intelligence 192
transactional theory 164
transfer 150
trial-and-error learning see instrumental
  learning
Triplett, Norman 102
Turner, John 104
Tversky, Amos 126, 127

valence 160, 161
Value, Instrumentality, and Expectancy
  approach (VIE) 160–1
visual projection pathway 27
visual-spatial scratchpad 122
Vroom, Victor 160

Watson, J.B. 144
Watson selection task 129
W.E.I.R.D cultures 196
Wernicke, Karl 38
Wiesel, Torsten 110
willpower 166, 167
working memory 122–3

Yale model 92

Zajonc, Robert 102

Acknowledgments

The authors would like to thank Elizabeth J. Newton for writing Chapter 3: Life-span Psychology. The authors would also like to make the following dedications:

Christopher Sterling: For my son Alexander, for strength in adversity.

Daniel Frings: To Louise, Katherine, and Annabelle, for all the joy they bring into my life.

Picture Credits

Quantum Books Limited would like to thank the following for supplying the images for inclusion in this book:

7 Shutterstock/CLIPAREA l Custom media; 15 Shutterstock/MadamSaffa; 25 Wikimedia Commons; 27 Shutterstock/Alila Medical Media; 33 Shutterstock/nobeastsofierce; 39 SHEILA TERRY/SCIENCE PHOTO LIBRARY; 43 Shutterstock/stockshoppe; 45 Shutterstock/Iconic Bestiary; 49 Wikimedia Commons; 51 Shutterstock/EcoPrint; 55 Nature Reviews Genetics 15, 347–359 (2014)/Jeffrey Rogers and Richard A. Gibbs; 57: (left) Wikimedia Commons, (top right), Shutterstock/Kirsten Wahlquist, (bottom right) Shutterstock/Kirsten Wahlquist; 67 Shutterstock/con3d; 73 Shutterstock/RioPatuca; 93 Shutterstock/LuckyN; 123 Shutterstock/racorn; 147: SUSAN KUKLIN/SCIENCE PHOTO LIBRARY; 169, 173 Shutterstock/www.BillionPhotos.com; 193 Shutterstock/Marza; 195 Shutterstock/LanaN; 199 Sam Kellerman; 215 Shutterstock/ellepigraficaok; 221 Dr. Elizabeth Sowell/Sowell ER, Thompson PM, Welcome SE, Henkenius AL, Toga AW & Peterson BS. Cortical abnormalities in children and adolescents with attention deficit hyperactivity disorder. The Lancet, 2003; 362(9397):1699-1707; 223 Shutterstock/Designua; 225 Shutterstock/Cranach.

While every effort has been made to credit contributors, Quantum Books Limited would like to apologize should there have been any omissions or errors and would be pleased to make the appropriate corrections to future editions of the book.